LETS
GO
PUBLISH

GO United States of America!

The Constitution 4 Dummmies

Your first book to read to refresh your knowledge of the greatest laws of the land, & how our government works

Read <u>The Constitution 4 Dummmies</u> so you understand your rights & your freedoms, so that nobody in government can take them from you!

Learn about your rights and freedoms by reading The Constitution 4 Dummmies! It is the best thing you can do to understand your role in assuring our great form of government.

This book is the best starter book for anybody wanting to refresh their knowledge or learn about the government and its most basic structure and laws. This book is to help you be better prepared to react to the over-reach of corrupt politicians at the highest levels of government. Without the knowledge that you can gain easily in this book, for example, you might think that your representatives in Congress control you instead of vice-verse. Smart people do not let their freedoms be taken from them, and you have entered into the realm of the intelligent by learning about the fundamental laws of America from the founders onward. These are the laws that assure your freedom. This book presents them in an understandable and almost fun way.

Today more than ever with our President and Congress acting in a lawless fashion or permitting lawlessness to be the law of the land, Americans need to know our rights and the protections built into the basic framework of our government formed by the US Constitution. Why did we wait so long?

Just because powerful people choose to ignore our rights and freedoms does not mean we must endure tyranny. The first step of course is to understand the most basic written precepts in the Constitution. Reading this book is a must.

LETS GO PUBLISH

BRIAN W. KELLY

Referenced Material *: Standard Disclaimer: The information in this book has been obtained through personal and third party observations, interviews, and copious research. Where unique information has been provided or extracted from other sources, those sources are acknowledged within the text of the book itself or at the end of the chapter in the Sources Section. Thus, there are no formal footnotes nor is there a bibliography section. Any picture that does not have a source was taken from various sites on the Internet with no credit attached. If resource owners would like credit in the next printing, please email publisher.*

Published by: LETS GO PUBLISH!
Associate Editor   Brian P. Kelly ....
Email: info@letsgopublish.com ....
Web site   www.letsgopublish.com

Library of Congress Copyright Information Pending
Book Cover Design by Michele Thomas,

ISBN Information: The International Standard Book Number (ISBN) is a unique machine-readable identification number, which marks any book unmistakably. The ISBN is the clear standard in the book industry. 159 countries and territories are officially ISBN members. The Official ISBN For this book is on the outside cover:

The price for this work is:								**$12.88 USD**	
10	9	8	7	6	5	4	3	2	1

Release Date: June 2016

Dedication

To the entire McKeown Family.
(My mother's side of the family)

They have all stood there with me and I with them, as we seek the truth and continue our fight for our freedoms.

Acknowledgments

In every book that I write or edit, I publicly acknowledged all of the help that I have received from many sources. Some of these wonderful people are still on earth and others have made their way to heaven.

I would like to thank many people for helping me in this effort. I appreciate all the help that I received in putting this book together, along with the 66 other books from the past.

My printed acknowledgments were once so large that book readers needed to navigate too many pages to get to page one of the text. To permit me more flexibility, I put my acknowledgment list online at www.letsgopublish.com. The list of acknowledgments continues to grow. Believe it or not, it once cost about a dollar more to print each book.

Thank you all on the big list in the sky and God bless you all for your help.

Please check out www.letsgopublish.com to read the latest version of my heartfelt acknowledgments updated for this book. Thank you all!

In this book, I received some extra special help from many avid Notre Dame supporters including Bruce Ikeda, Dennis Grimes, Gerry Rodski, Wily Ky Eyely, Angel Irene McKeown Kelly, Angel Edward Joseph Kelly Sr., Angel Edward Joseph Kelly Jr., Ann Flannery, Angel James Flannery Sr., Mary Daniels, Bill Daniels, Robert Gary Daniels, Angel Sarah Janice Daniels, Angel Punkie Daniels, Joe Kelly, Diane Kelly, Brian P. Kelly, Mike P. Kelly, Katie P. Kelly, Ben Kelly, and Budmund (Buddy) Arthur Kelly.

Preface

Indeed we are citizens of a truly exceptional country. America is the exception to the rule, founded on principles of liberty and freedom and ruled by the people. The Founders knew that even the great Constitution they wrote might not be enough to keep knaves and scoundrels from subverting their work.

And so, today, over 225 + years after the Constitution, all is not perfect in America, but the principles of the Constitution are so sound and so powerful that even a knave politician cannot bring us under. The big concern of course is that if we don't smarten up, things will get a lot worse. I suspect that is why you are reading this book.

Our ailments are large and growing. Taxes are too high, elected officials are out of touch, government is too big, spending is out of control; the new healthcare program is a train wreck, the federal government is incompetent, the people have no voice in government, too many people are too lazy to hold government accountable, too many are on the take, and worse than that, the list of ailments is growing, not shortening.

Things are happening that are lawless. Just the other day, the leader of the free world, without the required permissions of the Congress, traded five terrorists for a POW who had deserted his unit in Afghanistan. The father praised Allah and that too was difficult to understand considering the negotiations with the Taliban.

Your intention no doubt in learning about the structure of America and its most fundamental laws in choosing to read this book if to help you understand why all this is happening. . Thank you. That is why Brian wrote it. I am betting that more sooner than later, you will better understand our great country and our great form of government—at least before the bad guys take it away.

This book is the best starter book for anybody wanting to refresh their knowledge or learn about the government of the United States of America and to be better prepared to react to the over-reach of today's corrupt politicians at the highest levels of government. Without the knowledge that you can gain easily in this book, for example, you might unknowingly be convinced by socialist progressives in the government that you have no rights, and you have no freedoms, and any of your permissions come from the government itself.

If you have been paying attention to what is going on in America today, you know we are in trouble. We have a busted economy, high unemployment, no jobs, and our basic rights to freedoms such as speech, religion, the press, and our right-to-bear-arms are being impinged upon. The Founders saw it as a civic duty for Americans to pay attention to our government so that we can avoid being chumps and being snookered by crooked politicians.

There are more issues than just those noted above, and we better fix them quickly while we still have a Constitution upon which to lean.

We are on the same side in this battle for the Constitution and for the survival of America. Together we can all help. We first must understand what is going on and we then must understand our rights as delivered in the Declaration of Independence, The Constitution, and the Bill of Rights.

My concern is that when we all wake up from our deep fog, there may be no Bill of Rights or Constitution left for our progeny. We will have blown it for sure if that is permitted to happen.

In this book, Kelly unabashedly recommends that we stop trusting government since it is clearly not working for our best interests. The sooner we can understand the threat from the

Left, the sooner we can move on to solving the problem for our values, our country, and our freedom.

The smarter we are, the more chance we have for success. Understanding America's founding and the founding documents, especially the Constitution and The Bill of Rights, is a sure way to become an American forever. I know you love America as I do.

Your author continually monitors what is happening to our government and he has written extensively on the major problems our country faces. Brian Kelly is one of America's most outspoken and eloquent conservative spokesmen. He is the author of America 4 Dummmies, The Bill of Rights 4 Dummmies, No Amnesty! No Way!, The Lifetime Guest Plan, Saving America, Taxation Without Representation, , Kill the EPA!, Jobs! Jobs! Jobs!, The Federalist Papers by the Framers, and many other patriotic books. All books are available at www.bookhawkers.com.

Like many Americans, Brian is fed up with stifling socialist progressive Marxists in the top seats in Washington. They place the needs of everybody else in front of the needs of Americans. Like many Americans, Kelly is shocked at how brazen the administration is today in ignoring our Constitution and our Bill of Rights! This must be stopped.

Brian W. Kelly has read the founding documents, the underlying intelligence reports, and he has researched and written about such topics for years. Brian has written fifty-three books and hundreds of patriotic articles. He is deeply concerned about how intolerable the results of poor government policy can be within our neighborhoods and our lives. His comprehensible and sane recommendations in this book are explained in detail within the covers of this soon-to-be classic edition.

The Constitution 4 Dummmies! is a title to get your attention for sure. I hope we got your attention. In addition to a review of the founding history, your author has included a major civics lesson in this book to bring you up to date on the national scene. Additionally, he has included copies of the founding documents so that you can read them directly in this book, rather than on the Internet.

You are going to love this book since it is designed by an American for Americans. Few books are a must-read but The Constitution 4 Dummmies will quickly appear at the top of America's most read list.

Sincerely,

Brian P. Kelly, Editor

Table of Contents

About the Author

Brian W. Kelly retired as an Assistant Professor in the Business Information Technology (BIT) program at Marywood University, where he also served as the IBM i and midrange systems technical advisor to the IT faculty. Kelly designed, developed, and taught many college and professional courses. He is a contributing technical editor to a number of IT industry magazines. On the Patriotic side, you can once could find many Kelly article on www.conservativeactionalerts.com, which no longer is in business. These fine articles have been preserved on www. brianwkelly.com

Kelly is a former IBM Senior Systems Engineer and he has been a candidate for US Congress and the US Senate from Pennsylvania. He has an active information technology consultancy. He is the author of 67 books and numerous articles. Ask Brian speak at your next rally! You might be surprised!

Over the past nine years, Brian Kelly has become one of America's most outspoken and eloquent conservative protagonists. Besides The Constitution 4 Dummmies, Kelly is also the author of many other patriotic books. Check them out at www. bookhawkers.com, CreateSpace, and Kindle.

Part I Why Is This Book Necessary Today?

Chapter 1

Americans Are Mad as Hell About Government!

How mad can one get?

In case you missed it in my last book, the first of the 4 Dummies series-- America 4 Dummmies!, we're going to start out exactly the same way here but we will quickly get on to the meat of the US Constitution, the most wonderful document other than the Bible itself from the hand of God, that has ever been written. In essence, Americans are upset today because our Constitution is under attack.

The Constitution, the law of the land which you are about to explore, is unlawfully being bypassed by opportunists in government. That makes a lot of US "Mad as Hell!" Howard Beale in the paragraphs below represents all frustrated Americans. His story, though unrelated, really captures the mood and the emotions of America today regarding a government gone bad!

You may not remember because you are probably not old enough but many others of you have enough years to have seen the movie long after its debut in 1976. So, if you have some baggage, and you have some time on your bones, you may remember back in November, 1976 when Howard Beale, as played by Peter Finch, the long-time anchor in the movie

"Network News," gets the bad news that eventually causes him to utter one of the most famous movie lines of all time.

Beale gets fired and is given two weeks. The long-time anchor has a very poor reaction to this news and he cannot control himself during the next news broadcast.

He promises to commit suicide on the air. The company immediately fires him—no second chances for a repeat performance. Beale is devastated and remorseful. He begs for the opportunity to say good-by to his fans with dignity, and he is given his last opportunity ever for air time so that he can say his good-by's and also apologize. He gets his chance

Yet, once on the air, Beale is overwhelmed by his continuing circumstance. He goes into another diatribe starting off with a rant claiming that "Life is bullshit." He is so passionate that his ratings spike as he persuades his viewers to shout out of their windows: "I'm as mad as hell, and I'm not going to take this anymore!" That is the line heard 'round the world.

Well, my fellow Americans, I bet you saw this coming, and I am going to deliver it as passionately in words as I can: "I am mad as hell, and I am not going to take this anymore." I bet you are too. Let me remind you.

Taxes are too high, elected officials are out of touch, government is too big, spending is out of control, the Affordable Healthcare has become a train wreck, and heroes are dying in the VA system, and nobody, after spending $160 billion per year supposedly on Veterans, can tell us why they are neglected.

The people of America see the federal government as incompetent. We Americans have no voice. We exchange five top Taliban Officers from Gitmo for one PFC. Additionally, and this is the worst: too many of US are too lazy to hold government accountable, and too many of our finest are on the take.

It really is a train wreck. Corporate leaches have infiltrated our government. We have record unemployment, illegal aliens are smiling as they take American jobs; an unsustainable status quo supports special interests over the people's interests and when we look to the future we see a public education system that creates dummmies. The graduates are so dummm that they don't seem to mind being called dummmies. Scrooge would sum it up with a hearty "Bah Humbug." It is that bad!

We have the poorest economy since the depression, excessive welfare and income redistribution; institutionalized lying; a corrupt stat-loving press carrying water for government; a debt large enough to kill America; huge student debt stopping graduates' successes; tyranny v. democracy; government lawlessness; freedom and liberty in jeopardy; American stagnation, and a big loss of America's world prestige.

And, on top of that, the press beats its breast about its importance by suggesting that the president learns about what's happening across the world from reading the newspapers. Everybody in Washington gets a free ride with no accountability. It is that bad.

Our big government has become such a problem that most Americans believe that it can never again be the solution. Our finest hope, our youth; go through colleges in huge numbers only to be unemployed and sacked with debt for life. As a Democrat, I am smarter than most. I know that the Democratic Party is the source of their ill fortune. But, millennials do not believe it so they are not willing to fight the bad guys to make America great again!

This group of youngins known as millennials are the smartest by cranium but they are the stupidest offspring America has ever produced from anybody's loins in terms of their gullibility and their willingness to sacrifice their future for a promising promise.

They have no clue what life is about and they actually protest American heroes such as Condoleezza Rice and Dr. Ben Carson. Both came to visit universities and were disrespected by the students. Rutgers for example in 2013 picked a boardwalk babe, Snooki, rather than an American who loves America to give them their final addresses at their Universities. Hope is reserved for people who have never met today's millennials.

Students are guided by communists professors in universities and the students now accept that communism is OK. These are the elite progressives in their universities who believe free speech cannot be tolerated and who fill the heads of the millennials with mush. Their importance is endorsed by the universities when they get to be adorned in their finest plumage at commencement ceremonies, and they process before all others to the stage. With such guidance, students have learned that they really do know it all, though their parents have no clue what happens to them on campus.

In 2014 on through 2016, the administrators and the progressive / communist faculty and student lemmings at a once respected university named Rutgers, embarrassed conservative speakers including a fine American, Dr. Condoleezza Rice. Rice was scheduled to be commencement speaker. She is a major US historical figure besides being an academic in her own right.

The students, faculty, and administration were nasty and unwelcoming to her and they protested her choice as commencement speaker. Rice appropriately rescinded her acceptance. The children have taken over guided by the communists. Parents need to understand what is happening on campuses across the nation.

The student loan burden prevents former student borrowers from buying homes, cars, and having a family. Yet students do not blame their elite faculty and their establishment universities for anything. They blame George Bush for everything still because some talk show host once told them that works for him. It is great to have brains today, it is just not respected if one decides to use them for the public good.

Only retirees in their 90's can afford honeymoon cottages while looking for their next spouse. As many as 37 million student loan borrowers are too broke to engage in basic life. College loans, instead of lifting people to the top, have created a new race to the bottom,

On the International stage, America is a bad actor, and frustrated zealots from the left are making sure nobody gives America a break on the world stage. The US now seems to want to make the rest of the world strong by making America weak. The weaknesses of America are highlighted by a corrupt press because Americans have been doing too well and their perspective because of white privilege.

None of this helps command respect for our country from anybody but the guilt-ridden university students and their "lucky to have a job" mentors on the faculty. Having been a faculty member, I know how bad things are. The only people who seem to care have names like John Q. Public. Thank you John for choosing this book about the US Constitution.

Nobody in the world gives America standing ovations anymore. Nobody asks us for curtain calls. Our leaders turn their backs on our friends and seem to pay homage to our enemies. How is this? In mid-2014, we gave up five top command level terrorists from Gitmo for a POW who was a PFC when captured and promoted twice while in captivity. The POW is accused of desertion, and the Congress accused the administration of not following the law in the exchange. Has Congress lost all its power? Who has the power in the US? The Constitution says it is the people!

Smaller and weaker countries such as Russia, Iran, and North Korea continue to push US around and laugh at US, and our only response is to see if somehow it might have been because we may have offended them.

We show our greatness by counting the number of hits on a *hashtag of **bring our girls home,*** when no Americans are missing, and we expect terrorists to cower when the number of twitter resends hits a million.

We also refuse to have an honest discussion about why four Americans, including the US Ambassador, were permitted to die in Benghazi when the military says they were prepared to save them. The then Secretary of State responsible for their deaths is then able to run for President as if their deaths did not matter.

We have an administration that blames the Christian Government of Nigeria for not reaching out enough to the Muslim killers who kidnapped 300 girls for sex slaves. Boko Haram had captured and killed 49 boys just a few weeks before.

The captors boldly announced they would sell them on the sex slave market, and the US is powerless in its feeble response. The new strategy is to have time go by so those who are at fault can claim that it is old news.

What has happened to our good sense? Should there not be a set of laws written by sane people so that insane acts cannot occur without retribution? Why do our representatives, especially Republicans who have lots heart not represent America?

For me, these are the worst days of America that I have ever witnessed. Yet, our government seems to have no problems that need solutions. Clear-thinking Americans look at today's leaders as buffoons, without the wherewithal to tie their own shoes. We yearn for a guy like Donald Trump to come forth to save us. These leaders would like all Americans to be happy in a state of mediocrity, rather than being outstanding. "Don't worry: Be Happy!"

If you have been paying attention, and I sure hope you have been as it is a civic duty, you know that there are even more issues than the exhaustive list we just walked you through. Isn't that a shame on US? I think this is the reason that you bought this book. Thank you very much. The Constitution is a survivor's guide to dealing with a corrupt nation; a corrupt press; a corrupt government and corrupt politicians who believe they can trick you into finding them acceptable.

Since you bought this book, I know you and I are on the right side and thankfully we are on the same side. Together, we can all help arrest control of our government back from perpetrators wishing to destroy US.

We first must understand what is going on and we then must understand our rights. Even before you and I and everybody else are on board, just like Howard Beale, we must start the first wave of solutions by opening our windows all the way and shouting as loud as we all can: "I am mad as hell, and I am not going to take this anymore."

Then, make sure that you talk to all of the other "dummmies" out there that you know—people like you and I and others, and let's help them know that unless we all fully engage in America, when we wake up from our deep fog, there may be no America left for our progeny. We will have blown it for sure if that is permitted to happen.

Chapter 2

The USA is a Constitutional Republic!

A Representative Democracy

The Constitution prescribes that the US is a representative democracy, which as you will see, along with having an elected chief executive and a constitution also makes the US a *Republic*. The pledge of allegiance notes the words: "…and to the *Republic* for which it stands," for our country is both a representative democracy and a republic.

When we think of the very important notion that "America is a representative democracy," watching the "clowns" from both parties who occupy our central government, it is a sane question to ask if this is really true.

The song, "Is that all there is?" comes to mind. We are nothing like our parents and nothing like our Founders. We have reason to be ashamed of our government, but then again, our country today is so far off the Founders' mark that even shame is not politically correct.

A representative democracy is the foundation of America. However, what makes America—America is that we are also a Republic, the finest form of government ever brought forth from mankind.

We also have a set of laws, beginning with our Constitution, the primary law of the land. These laws govern all people and all politicians in perpetuity—as long as we hold them accountable.

The simple definition of a republic (from Latin -- res publica, meaning is as follows: a state in which supreme power is held by the people and their elected representatives, and which has an elected or nominated president rather than a monarch.

In practice in a republic, the government is ruled by elected leaders run according to law. The law in our country is The Constitution. Unlike a democracy, a republic is not based on majority rule. The law of the land, a Constitution gives the minority a voice.

Our biggest and most important laws within the US Constitution are written so that the government cannot hurt the people (US) or impose its will upon US. Our country was founded by some very smart people and they knew that without constraints on any government, which could potentially go wild, the people would not be able to win.

The constraints in the Constitution are implicit in that all of the rights are owned by the people, and only those rights explicitly given to government are for the government. In our time from 2014 to 2016, and for most of the Obama years. The people's rights have not counted. Obama's rights as an apparent dictator have been what has mattered. Even Republicans back down fearing Obama as an instrument of the people. In 2016, the full body of people in the US have gotten fed up with Obama and Hillary Clinton and all of the dishonest politicians in America. Though the press and the esteemed Republican establishment tell the people that Donald Trump is not worth their vote, the people have rejected the establishment on both sides and Donald Trump is the only good guy in town. God bless him in his victory!
0

This great body of law known as the Constitution, therefore makes politicians and others in government fear a backlash when they attempt to deny the people, even just one person our liberty and freedom. In a pure democracy, if the majority decided that you or I should be killed, nothing would necessarily stop it. But, in a republic, our form of government, it is the rule of law which prevails and the rule of law starts with the Constitution. The current president unfortunately does not like the rule of law.

It seems for sure that many in our nation today, mostly on the far left, are trying real hard to kill America's America by demeaning the Constitution and the Bill of Rights in particular. You more than likely selected this book to help fight them off. Thank you.

If you could figure any way to put an unmovable grip on corrupt politicians, right now or in the future, would you not do it? The founders of America put such a stranglehold on all political agents of the future when they wrote and adopted the US Constitution, the greatest body of law ever written in any civilization.

Of course, if we the people do not know what is written in the Constitution, it cannot help us much. Can it? So, it is time for all Americans who have not been paying attention to stop being dummmies and political sport for the elite. It is time to rule America as our birthright as citizens of this great country commands US. Let somebody else eat cake!

And, so, my fellow Americans, that is the number one reason that in order to form a more perfect union of the original thirteen colonies / states, and with more states expected after the first thirteen, our forefathers built the finest Constitution ever fashioned by the pen of human hands.

The Bible, from the hand of God, may be the greatest story ever told in the greatest book ever written, but the Constitution is as good as it gets for the goodness of man, written by the hands of our first patriots, and surely this document was written with the guidance of God.

In this day and age, there are everyday attempts by the government to undermine our lasting Republic, which is an almost pure constitutional representative democracy. The attacks most often come from the left side of the political spectrum. Democrats can be better patriots for sure.

Democracy is the opposite of communism

The ideology of the progressive left favors Marxism and its simpler forms of socialism and communism. Since Americans do not typically vote for socialists, communists, or Marxists, other than some who vote for Bernie Sanders rather than crooked Hillary, these are things that nobody other than a crooked politician should want.

If you are unaware of this in today's government, it is time you considered paying more attention. No politician wanting to be elected will admit they are more communist than American. Yet, as much as it pains me to tell you, unfortunately, they are!

These overtures, which demean the Constitution, the fabric of our democracy, originate from corrupt politicians who have been caught up in a leftist movement, which would like to end capitalism, and bring on a socialist / communist order to replace the American Dream, and all the dreams of *We the People*!

Our Republic as noted is a representative democracy constrained by laws. The Constitution is the biggest constraint that prohibits government from taking over—and that is good. Yet, we do have representatives.

One midnight, I asked myself one of those haunting questions: "Isn't it about time that we real Americans actually had some real "representation" from the so-called representatives in our so-called representative government? I said to myself: "Yes it is!" It doesn't have to be a dream.

If we believe, it can easily again be made a reality. And, we should scream it out at the polling places and at our representative's offices as often as we can. We should accept nothing less. Americans rule America. It is our birthright given to us by the founders.

The people have the responsibility of keeping government honest!

It is up to all people in this great country to understand our laws, first the Constitution, and then to pay attention that our leaders follow those laws. When the top officials in our government do not follow the laws of the land, we must learn to send them home every two, four, or six years, as determined by the term lengths as set forth in the Constitution for our House (2 years), the President (4 years), and the Senate (6 years) respectively.

To say it more clearly: We get to throw the bums out and replace them with people of character on a regular basis; so don't give up! Donot let the politicians think they run the country! That is why our government has worked well for over 225 years. When we get bad apples, we throw them away by voting them out. Of course that means we must vote in order for our choices to matter. And we must be willing to vote our own representatives in the House or the Senate out of office when they choose to not do their jobs.

Representatives are of the people?

Though the representatives are supposed to come from the people, a type of political class of elites has come about and seldom do we get to vote for representatives anymore, who are truly representatives of the people. By understanding America better, and especially by understanding our Constitution, Americans have a far better chance of bringing good and honest government back to the people. We must not be afraid of casting out the evil politicians in our government.

The way it now works, there is far too much separation between US, the electors, and them, the elected officials. Most officials choose to live in gated communities, unaware of what is happening on our streets.

The Constitution provides that elected officials are given the task to coordinate our pooled resources for the intended benefit of "everyone." But everyone is often not included. And politicians often take credit for spending treasury dollars on things that simply buy themselves votes. Nobody wants this and so it is up to all of US to change it.

Do our representatives in the second decade of the twenty-first century have a genuinely compelling concern for the people and our government or is this simply our notion of Nirvana? We know that Nirvana is the name in Buddhism as its final goal—a transcendent state in which there is neither suffering, desire, nor sense of self; and the subject is released from the effects of karma and the cycle of death and rebirth.

If it is not Nirvana, perhaps it is a Disney-like Utopian myth perpetrated on US by these same "benevolent politicians?" Of course, it may be that our representatives do not care because we do not hold them accountable. We elect them even when they are knaves—even thieves and criminals. Do any of US think politicians really care about the people?

I propose the latter. Our government is wholly unaccountable to We the People. Today, our government rejects the fundamental principles of our founding and has no real legitimacy the further it drifts from the precepts of the Constitution.

The US was not designed this way. The Constitution is the blueprint for our Country's design. It was designed by a group of artisans to not only represent their artistic touch, but to be held as the behavioral creed of the people, for the people, and by the people, forever. What thinking human being blessed to be part of America, could ask for anything more?

If you think that life, freedom, liberty, and the ability to pursue your own happiness are simple notions, and givens in any civilization, get out your thinking cap, and think again. Why do people from all over the world crash our gates just to get in? Americans are exceptional in that we have full freedom and liberty in our country, and with that we can exceed all limits. Go to any other country, and this exception no longer applies.

Traditionally, the USA has been the freest nation in the world with rights withheld from government and rights given to the people by our Constitution. Today as our country's foundation is being threatened from within, more than likely you are reading about the Constitution so you can help protect your rights as well as this great nation which provides them.

Which would you first give up? Your freedom? Your life? Your liberty? Your family? Or your ability to do what you need to do to be happy? The sanest answer of course is "none of the above."

Who could ask for anything more than being an American? Ask the last arriving immigrant! We are free! But, if Americans do not care about our founding precepts, maybe our freedom, our lives, our liberty, our families, and our ability to do what we need to be happy, will be taken from us one day—perhaps in the not-too-distant future.

If the design of our nation, America, which the founders labored to create is so great, you might ask, why is it that our current lawmakers ignore it? Republicans and Democrats alike appear to be indifferent to the needs of the people they represent.

They have no trouble going with the flow and committing US to years of debt without even taking the time to read the debt-ridden legislation for which they vote. Neither the Constitution nor the Founders would approve of what our representatives, including our president, have done to our country.

Even worse, members of Congress, our alleged civil servants, are able to get away without doing their jobs, while collecting more and more remuneration for their main act of harming the American people at large.

The true answer to that question is very unfortunate for Americans. There is tacit collaboration in undermining the principles of our Democratic Republic by our supposed representatives, their supporters, the special interests, and their corporate interests. We the people now come last. They think we are not paying attention. Maybe we have not been paying enough attention but don't you agree that is about to end. Pay attention is about to become the motto of the free!

Legitimate immigration was necessary

Americans are all pro-immigration to the extent of our laws. If Americans were not pro-immigration for example, Columbus and his shipmates and their families more than likely would have withered away from disease or cold winters or they would have lost their battles with Native Americans. All fifty states; at least the mainland forty-eight, would probably now have Native American names, and they would be run by the same financial wizards who run today's highly successful casinos.

After the USA was in operation as a country with a Constitution for just several years, its population was approaching 4 million people. This is just a million more people than the annual flow of illegal immigrants from south of the border.

On March 26, 1790, almost 225 years ago, the second session of the first Congress (operating under the Constitution with a House and a Senate) approved the new nation's initial effort to create the rules under which foreign-born persons could become U.S. citizens.

From this point on, our borders were not open per se, and we had laws (rules) for how those wishing to be Americans could come to visit or to become Americans. All Americans after this point who immigrated were to follow the law of the land.

The Naturalization Act of 1790 specified that "any alien, being a free white person," could apply for citizenship, so long as he or she lived in the United States for at least two years, and in the state where the application was filed for at least a year. The new law also provided that "children of citizens of the United States that may be born ... out of the limits of the United States shall be considered as natural born citizens."

In effect, it left out indentured servants, slaves, and most women. It also mandated that one must "absolutely and entirely renounce and abjure all allegiance and fidelity to every foreign Prince, Potentate, State or Sovereignty." Though these terms were seen as quite generous, still the law denied the right to naturalize to "persons whose fathers have never been resident in the United States."

Immigration law was becoming more important and the laws have been changed several times since 1790. For example, in 1795, as anti-immigrant feeling began to grow, the necessary period of residence to become a citizen was increased from two to five years. Immigration law became more firm as the nation aged.

Enter special interests, who like to bypass laws and have their friendly "owned" politicians let them get away with whatever. Regarding immigration, you already know that there are two major special interests. The first special interest is the Democratic Party, which believes that if all illegal foreign nationals were immediately made citizens, the Democrat Party would never lose another election. That is a great motivator to bring all foreigners in immediately and make them all citizens of this nation.

And, so, even though they have taken American jobs and driven down the average weekly wage, your Democratic Representatives in Congress still advocate amnesty and citizenship for them, promising less prosperity for all American citizens. And, unfortunately, most Americans, not seeing that the representatives have become socialists and communists, looking for a poor continually underserved underclass, they will vote them back into office to their own peril.

Their major concern as corrupt politicians is that the Democrat members of Congress get reelected and a Democrat president can be elected each time. Bringing in poor people from south of the border, who feed from our welfare system, assures the Democratic politicians of their votes.

The second special interest is also against the people. They do not gain at the ballot box. However, illegal foreign nationals do provide huge gains in the wallets of American Business. American businesses, represented today by the elite Republican establishment, love paying the smallest wage possible. Since illegal foreign nationals work for peanuts, this is a perfect marriage of needs.

Traditional Republicans have great alliances with businesses. The only groups, who align with the majority of Americans and who oppose blanket amnesty and who are 100% pro-American citizen philosophically, are conservatives, such as those who once claimed allegiance in the TEA Party. They differ on immigration with elitist Republicans, and opportunist Democrats. No American citizen suffering from the worst economy since the depression would be asking the government to invite in more wage lowering workers.

After Republicans chose to side with Democrats when becoming the majority in the house and senate, Tea Party advocates have gone underground in disgust. Many of the same people who once made up the tea party transformed from idealistic Tri-cornered hat wearing patriots who believed that Republican campaign rhetoric that mirrored their beliefs have changed their orientation. They have become a much more savvy and in some ways more cynical electorate. That is why Donald Trump is doing so well. The elitist establishment Republicans are held in poor regard.

Thomas J. Donahue, President of the US Chamber of Congress, a disgusting voice for the establishment told Republican lawmakers that if they did not pass amnesty, the Republicans shouldn't even bother to run a candidate in 2016. Populist conservatives go the message loud and clear that establishment Republicans could not be trusted.

 The C of C cares nothing about workers' salaries but cares a lot about corporate profits. Donohue demanded that lawmakers to pass amnesty rather than pass on funding from the Chamber for their reelections. Observing the establishment has begun to make populist conservatives suffer from nausea.

The US Senate, controlled by Democrats, passed a global amnesty bill in early 2014, and they were pressuring the House of Representatives to do the same. The conservatives in the House would not budge thankfully. Of course if they pass this scourge on America, just as Marco Rubio got beaten by Trump in 2016, the people will revolt and with no excuses left, throw out both houses of Congress and start over. The people have lots of power when we "pay attention."

The immigration issue is being put forth early in this book to demonstrate that our legislators care more about other factors such as reelection and donations than they do about the people. We have enough people in the country right now or else our real unemployment picture would not look so bad. Why bring more "slave labor" into the country when we know it will make the problem of making ends meet for American families that much worse?

Perhaps too many of US, until things got this bad, had been hoping George would do it! Well, George Washington, one of our finest patriots is long gone, and unless you know of a recent George with the time, it is up to US to do it. Those in Congress who bow to special interests and liberal instincts should be made to take their final bows.

And, by the way, the two George Bush's did not get it done either. But, today's President and his Attorney General don't even try. They are on the other team. They choose not to enforce any immigration law. They do not follow the law of the land, the Constitution. This is tyranny, yet with a Republic Congress that defers to the president, it is tough to get action on behalf of the people.

This book is not about immigration, but it is about the Constitution and the Bill of Rights. Both of these documents help all Americans to know that the laws are made for Americans to benefit. To demonstrate the lawlessness of the current administration and the disdain they have even for war heroes, here are a few anecdotes.

Without a scintilla of Constitutional authority, just recently, today's President ordered well over 30,000 imprisoned criminals in illegal status to simply be released so "they could be reunited with their families in the US." Among them are rapists and murderers. The homicide victims got no say. The criminals were released from prison into the US—not deported.

They are back on the streets of the US. Did we really need 30,000 more criminals on our streets? Today's President thinks we should cajole and love the 60,000,000 souls in our illegal population, and he acts like our laws do not apply to him or to foreigners. Meanwhile 30,000 American citizens in prison were not released to be with their families. I agree

American criminals should not be released but neither should foreign national criminals.

There is another true story that shows how ridiculous it is for the US to bend over backwards to coddle 30,000 criminals with illegal foreign national status. Mexican authorities know how to handle immigration. They punish Americans in Mexico for the smallest of infractions and will not free them even when there is national outrage in the USA. About a year ago, many of you may recall that Mexican authorities were holding Sergeant Andrew Tahmooressi, a Marine war hero from Florida.

US outrage was expressed in a headline from Memorial Day Weekend, 2014: "Leave no man behind: Why is Team Obama unable to bring home Marine held in Mexico?" Later many were wondering how today's president could free a deserter from the Taliban and completely ignore the plight of a hero marine.

While on the battlefield, this brave Marine saved eight fellow Marines from the Taliban, and in a separate incident he saved a Marine from bleeding to death after he stepped on an IED and lost his legs. Tahmooressi also suffered a concussion when his vehicle hit an IED.

On March 20, 2014, the U.S. Department of Veterans Affairs diagnosed this young soldier with Post-Traumatic Stress Disorder (PTSD). Yet, even our President cannot get him freed from a Mexican Jail. Maybe the President has not yet made the call, or maybe he simply does not like Marines? Or maybe he has no power? Who really knows?

This unlucky former Marine simply mis-navigated the San Diego highways and ended up in Mexico. Rather than being treated with respect and returned, this hero Marine was apprehended and incarcerated and after two to three months, he was still there fearing for his life in a dreadful and very dangerous Mexican prison.

After a night in which he avoided death from a prison "Hit Squad," he was placed in solitary confinement with his four limbs chained to a bed. We treat no illegal foreign nationals with such cruelty. Maybe Mexico is trying to teach the US how to treat border violators?

Can it be that too many of US and too many of our friends have been constitutional dummmies for too long? Perhaps understanding our rights and government limitations from the Constitution, as well as your exhortations to all your friends will help many Americans awaken to what happens in a country in which government, rather than the people, has the stronger hand.

Chapter 3

Why Does The Constitution Matter?

Americans are too trustworthy

Our representatives are in office far too long and they gain relationships with other politicians who make up the ruling class. Instead of thinking about the folks in Danbury or Wilkes-Barre, or Clarks-Summit, or Santa Rosa, or Chicago, or Avoca, or Great Plains, or Orlando, our esteemed politicians begin to think they belong in Washington DC, not their home cities.

The social life in DC is lots better than most home towns, and our devoted representatives get to rub elbows with the hoity-toity, and the progressive Marxist communists that do not exist in their home areas. They get corrupted. All of a sudden they are important, and being from Podunk or Plymouth does not matter. They begin to like the trappings of Washington more than being with their loved ones back in their home states.

And they try to please the lobbyists and the communists and even those on the other team. They want to be liked and they want something in return that they don't get from the home town folks. Sometimes it is gifts, sometimes it is invitations to the best parties, and sometimes it is the promise of a great job if not reelected. The longer they are in Congress or in politics per se, the greater the opportunity for corruption.

Unfortunately for all Americans, the new "important" relationships trump the notion of fair representation for the people (US) from back home. When they take their oaths of office and they promise to represent US, most are sincere at the time. That may be the last time.

Once they come to Washington, they experience the trappings and the temptations. And, because humans are only human, way too many of our finest stray from the mark and contribute to the re-creation of a country of which few thinking Americans are proud today.

Yet, we Americans are either too kind or not enough self-assured that we trust them even after innumerable lies and self- aggrandizement. We can't believe they would do "that," yet they do. So, like dummies, we go ahead and we call them hizzoner or herronner and we reelect them because we think they really cannot be that bad.

Ladies and gentlemen, they are that bad. Stop electing them. Their biggest fear is that someday all Americans will understand the Constitution chapter and verse. On that day, we have all the rights, and they have zero.

Think about our Forefathers, especially George Washington, who guided our troops in the revolution against England's tyranny. Think about honest Abe Lincoln, who freed the slaves and saved the union. They would weep to see what their political successors, our representatives, have done to our nation.

So, our fair haired representatives (figure of speech) choose to represent themselves and their special interests, rather than the areas of the country that sent them to the Congress of the USA to represent the people. Perhaps a dose of Lincoln's "honesty," is all that is needed to save the day. Wouldn't that be nice?

Our "honorable," do not even seem to care for our well-being. They do, however, care for their leadership positions, which make them big shots. They care for themselves for sure. Unfortunately, they just can't get it into their heads that we the people are the reason they are in their positions in the first place.

We the people are the employers of all members of Congress, and they serve at our pleasure. The more we all understand that the tighter the reins we can place on errant politicians, the more the people are in charge. It is not too late. The Constitution is our guide and it is our license to rid ourselves of a poor government.

We must understand the Constitution in order for it to work again for US and for America. The last thing we should consider doing is to permit corrupt politicians that we unfortunately have already elected to serve the people, to disembody our Constitution through legislation or through executive actions.

Part of the problem is our fault since we do not check them out well enough before we slam them into office. To make it simple to understand this notion—if there is a rotten piece of fish in the market and we select it for dinner, whose fault is it when it doesn't taste so good and our guests get sick? So, when we pick a rotten person to represent US—whose fault is that? You see, we do not have to be dummmies. We simply choose to be.

Does it matter whether the government is controlled by Democrats or Republicans? Democratic leaders have become socialist progressives, just this side of communists over the past several years. The Democrats at home are not far leftists but their leaders are. Republicans still seem to love the American way and are not moving the country towards communism. But, Republicans are too passive in dealing with

Democratic leadership that appears hell-bent on destroying our country.

Our country's demise rate grows at a higher rate when leftist progressive communists are in office. When Republicans take over, though it lessens, it does not go to zero as it should because a number of Republicans have become progressive also.

So, right now at least, Republicans, especially conservative Republicans are a better choice for America than Democrats. As a conservative Democrat myself, that is very tough for me to say. I wish it were not so. The best thing for America is to vote for conservatives, even if they are Democrat. But, the facts show most conservatives are either Republican or Libertarian.

The people have been short-changed on the notion of representation and honesty. Honesty is the first thing to go when a representative must lie in order to get the extra benefits their positions can deliver.

When has any incumbent representative run effectively on honesty? Is that because we the people do not care about honesty or are we all smart enough to know that they are kidding. We do not need the Constitution to know that but it might help us to be more honest if we knew and loved the Constitution just a little bit more. Either way it is our fault. We voted all of these 545 miscreants to run our government. We get the government we deserve.

Somebody once said that if you like your honesty, you will be able to keep it and it should save you about $2500.00 per year. Do you remember who that guy was? He was talking bout us all saving $2500 on Obamacare policies. How'd that work out for you? Helping fight a guy like that is a great place in which we can use our knowledge of the Constitution.

Nobody said that exactly but some president at some time in the last several years did tell Americans that we could keep our doctors, health policies, and that in so doing we would save at least $2500.00. I am not kidding. He still tells lies because no person in Congress feels strong enough to take him on.

My objective in this book as in many others, which I write, is not to have you know who said that or to get you upset whether he or she did or did not say it. I just want you to think about what the Founders promised and what American government had been delivering to the people before the liars took charge of the government. There is a chasm. We the people can fix that. Learning the precepts of the Constitution can inspire US to get that task done.

My objective is to help smarten you up so that guys like that, whether they are the president or not, do not get to treat you like a chump. Each time I write about this topic, I get smarter also as we all must keep learning all our lives and we must be watchful to keep our freedoms.

America is built on fairness, goodness, and individual strength. We are not supposed to give politicians an even break. The Constitution is our law and it is our obligation to pay attention so our rights are not violated by grabby politicians. If you happen to be in this low information / overly nice category, thank you for visiting this book. I hope that through these writings, you will become a better American.

The low information gullible people in America must smarten up or we are all toast. Everybody's vote counts the same. When those who choose to not pay attention vote, it is a big plus for dirty politicians and a big loss for real Americans.

When you have the time, please finish reading this book, and you will understand how smart you can be and how much power you can wield against those who care nothing about you or me, or America. Always keep your eye on the ball and do not give the ball up to an opponent just because they lie and they schmooze you.

The Constitution 4 Dummmies, is written so that we can all know the truth even when the corrupt media lie to our faces. The not-so-free, very dishonest and corrupt press provides cover for the government as an ally, not as the fourth estate. It is propaganda for the government and too many gullible Americans sop it up as if it is the truth. The media would have us all believe in the "*Tooth Fairy.*" Any of US that live by believing their lies, need to reevaluate so that we do not remain chumps.

Regardless of which party is responsible for the mess, Americans are on edge anticipating that somehow, because there are big problems, we will all get nailed by one or another of them in one way or another. Many of US think that we will lose our jobs, lose our ability to work full time, lose our health insurance policies, and not be able to afford the new government issued policies coming our way.

When I was growing up, it was not this way. It is time we went back to the better days when there was a real American Dream for everybody. .

We may get sick and we may die because of the "Affordable Care Act." Thank God the president is not under Obamacare so at least he will be available for a eulogy at any of our funerals.

Illegal immigration and amnesty is another of the bad jokes perpetrated on the American people. In this instance, both the Democrats and the Republicans share the same vision – *to stiff the American people,* and to give priority to illegal foreign nationals rather than American citizens. What happened to America and Americans first?

We discussed this topic in detail in Chapter 2. Some truths stand forever. Even today's president, when he met with Pope Francis could not think of anything positive to say, so he quoted his buddy Harry Reid as you can see in the "cartoon" below. The bubbled exchange with the Pope is funny but too true. Pope Francis must have a great sense of humor. Don't we just love his simplicity?

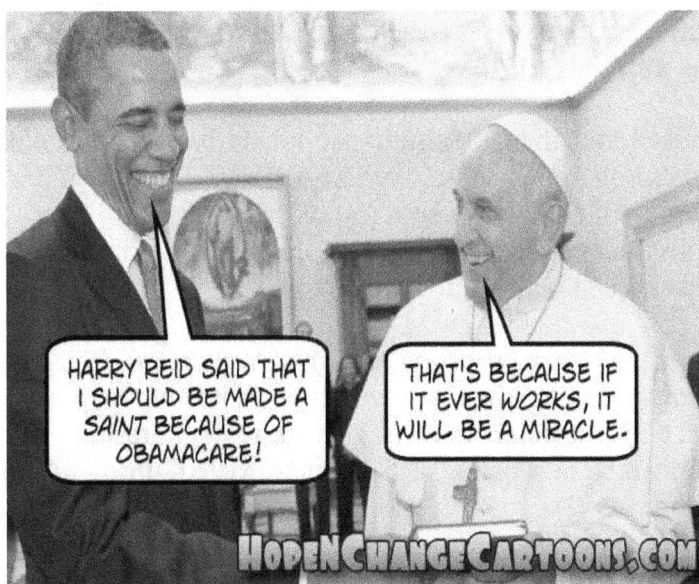

And, so, I decided that this book about the US Constitution would not be too political and it shall not be. It is anti-political. But, we must tell the truth about how things really are—don't you think?

I have admitted previously that I am a registered Democrat but for twenty years or more, I have not been proud of my Party. The Democratic Leadership can do a lot better. Right now the Party that is the lesser of two evils is unquestionably the Republican Party though it is an unholy combination of both Democrats and Republicans that have given us this sad state of affairs in the USA.

To help you and your family cope with the times, this book will be truthful and fact-filled and it will make each political party seem like they, and they alone, along with the two party system—are responsible for the problems that America has been suffering while it is trying to stay America.

I know that when you and I think about it, we are on the same page for the same reason. We are all trying to preserve the American way of life—which cannot be found anywhere else in the universe.

Because I love the Constitution so much, I wrote this book so that I can share my sense of what America really is, and why, until the millennials got shut out of the American dream, with no jobs after college; this was the place in which anybody could succeed with some hard work.

America not only promised an American Dream. It delivered. And during that time, the government followed the precepts of the Constitution. Today as government ignores the American Dream or suggests it never existed, life simply is not as good.

Do not accept the communist doctrine that this is the new normal. They want to dummm you down and then take your freedoms. We can do much better and we will. It all starts by paying attention.

I hope this book helps to wake up Americans of all ages from the fog that has affected our brains. We have not changed but we have permitted our government to change. Our representatives and our government has changed so much that they have forgotten who we are and who we are supposed to be.

Without using those exact words, our Constitution gives us a government of the people, by the people, and for the people. It gives government only powers that are specifically enumerated by the people. Yet, somehow, Americans have become lazy and we have permitted corrupt politicians to be reelected regardless of whether they represent US well or not.

Abraham Lincoln is the most famous historical figure to use this patriotic phrase. It was in his Gettysburg Address from November 19, 1863. For posterity, here is Lincoln's last paragraph. It is chilling:

"It is rather for us to be here dedicated to the great task remaining before us -- that from these honored dead we take increased devotion to that cause for which they gave the last full measure of devotion -- that we here highly resolve that these dead shall not have died in vain -- that this nation, under God, shall have a new birth of freedom -- and that government of the people, by the people, for the people, shall not perish from the earth."

Big government doesn't work. Big agencies don't work. Big corporations don't work. Big doesn't work well at all, especially if you are one person looking for freedom and liberty.

Government has grown so big that we the people, who own the government according to a deed known as the Constitution, can no longer sort through all the lies and the empty promises. So, we must all help reduce the size of government for the people to ever matter again. We get our chances each election cycle. When we vote to favor corruption, we get the government we deserve.

If all Americans understood America, and were taught to respect America in our schools, instead of blaming America first for everything—we would not have to worry about being defeated from within.

In this way, if any American political party comes-by led by Democrats or Republicans, and it wants to change America into a Communist-Russian-like, or Communist-Chinese-like, or Nazi-German-like country, we will be equipped to fire off a quick nyet, or a mhai, or simply, a hearty and guttural nein!

We can surely add no-way Jose for effect if we choose, simply because we are Americans and we are exceptional. We are the exception to the rule that freedom and liberty cannot work with regular people. What we cannot do is accept and believe the propaganda from the corrupt, socialist progressive communist owned press in the US. Yes, that includes the New York Times, the Washington Post and of course MSNBC. Trying to find the truth in today's news is like trying to find a white glove in the snow.

America, from its inception, along with mercantilism, has used capitalism to create the strongest country in the world. Those who do not like America have already removed mercantilism from the landscape and now hope to replace capitalism with socialism / communism. Yet, small-c-communism has never worked anyplace.

Their replacement scenario is a promise of the best of small "c" communism in our later evolution, or revolution, but they may not permit freedom lovers to live when they gain control, if we are not totally happy with their form of control.

If you believe in any of these socialist philosophies and you also like your freedom, it might be a good time to visit the tombstone makers in your area and pick out a good one. In memoriam! You are gone!

Chapter 4

The Founders Wrote the Constitution to Protect US from Tyranny

Socialism, progressivism, Marxism, and communism were considered but rejected

America has always been a capitalist country in which hard work pays off, and the same goes for our economy. If any American political party comes-by led by Democrats or Republicans, and it wants to change America into a communist, socialist, or Marxist country, once you understand the Constitution, and you are no longer part of the dummmy crowd, you will be well-equipped with the information you are absorbing in this book to fire off a resounding "NO" in our native language of English.

Many of the founders, and our relatives from long ago, risked their lives to engage George III of England so America could be free. I mean so that the people could be free and have unbounded liberty. Nobody of sane mind at the time wanted a revolution, but they eventually agreed that freedom is worth a revolution and a free America proves it every day.

Those from countries other than England who came to America engaged other Kings and royalty in addition to King George III. But, all came to America to be free. All

Americans in the twenty-first century need to wake up to realize that freedom is not free.

The Founders never envisioned that tyranny would come from the people itself or from the supposed independent press, the so-called fourth estate. The press is known as the fourth estate, an entity whose job has always been to keep government honest. Today that's like enlisting a weasel to guard the hen house.

The true role of the free press is not to take sides with corporations or government or any party. It is not to bring in the most ad revenue and tell falsehoods as if they were fact. Yet, we have no fourth estate today in America because our press leans communist, and they back every word of the administration as if they are a branch of the Democratic Party.

The Founders never expected the citizenry to stand by and permit the powerful to take away liberties for which the revolutionaries shed blood. Our founders would not be happy with many of US today, because we sit idly and let things happen to US.

These brave souls said no to the repression of freedom and they took matters into their own hands, risking life and limb, to provide US all with a free America. In this country, all of the people are free. Go get yourself a breath of fresh air. It is free. Only the corrupt press today will tell you to pay homage to something or somebody to get your clean air.

Today, it is a phenomenon that the well-to-do politicians have become very popular with the dummmest of Americans, who want what they can give to them. Today's politicians, disguised as representatives of the people are sharp and cunning, and they are always ready to say or do anything that would help them advance to important offices of the city, the state or in the federal government.

The word "politician" is used in the book in its most derisive form and always un-complimentary. Who are politicians? Politicians of the worst order are scoundrels who gain the people's trust and get elected to office and then they turn on the people for their own self-interests. Today they dupe the lowest level of information citizens and they tease them with handouts to gain control of them.

The founders were well aware of politicians in England and other countries in Europe, and the treachery they caused. Back in the late 1700's as the Constitution was prepared for ratification, the founders were so tickled that George III was no longer in control, they almost universally felt that the new America, which they were creating, would remain pure over time. Who would ever give up freedom?

Using the Constitution, they tried to build a set of laws that would never ever, ever, require another popular revolution to purify the government. They knew there was the risk of scoundrels who may in later years attempt to take control of the government. In the twenty-first century, those scoundrels are here in droves, and the corrupt press has joined them to keep the people down.

That is why the founders rewrote the first Constitution known as the Articles of Confederation *"in order to form a more perfect union."* Though their work was excellent, scoundrels still flourish. The union under the Constitution is much more perfect than under the Articles of Confederation (the first iteration of national law); but it is not perfect enough to stop all scoundrels at the doorstep.

To understand that the Founders advocated dissolving and re-forming a government gone badly, this section of the Declaration of Independence does the trick:

"...That whenever any Form of Government becomes destructive of these ends, it is the Right of the People to

alter or to abolish it, and to institute new Government, laying its foundation on such principles and organizing its powers in such form, as to them shall seem most likely to affect their Safety and Happiness. Prudence, indeed, will dictate that Governments long established should not be changed for light and transient causes; and accordingly all experience hath shown that mankind are more disposed to suffer, while evils are sufferable than to right themselves by abolishing the forms to which they are accustomed. But when a long train of abuses and usurpations, pursuing invariably the same Object evinces a design to reduce them under absolute Despotism, it is their right, it is their duty, to throw off such Government, and to provide new Guards for their future security."

Though the Founders did not specifically add anything in the original constitution permitting the government to be overthrown by force, it is implicit as that is exactly what they did as leaders of America to answer Britain's tyranny.

Since the people have all rights in the Constitution, as you will see shortly, the Second Amendment to the constitution in the Bill of Rights provides all citizens the right to bear arms and it prohibits government from impinging on that right. And thus, the Declaration of Independence shows the willingness of the Founders to use force to overthrow a government if the government goes bad. Meanwhile, the 2nd Amendment gives the people the means – most notably guns and ammunition.

Ron Paul, Mark Levin, Andrew Napolitano and others see it exactly the same way as I do!

Ron Paul: *the Second Amendment, ironically, and a lot of people don't understand this, but it was to protect against abusive government.*

Mark Levin *said that the 2nd amendment wasn't for target shooting or hunting or anything else in that realm. He said that "whether you like it or not or whether you agree with it or not, the reason why 2nd amendment exists is to arm the* *population in order to overthrow a tyrannical government. That's it."*

Judge Andrew Napolitano: *The historical reality of the Second Amendment's protection of the right to bear arms is not that it protects the right to shoot deer. It protects the right to shoot tyrants, and it protects the right to shoot at them effectively with the same instruments they would use upon us.*

The fact that Americans are armed is unusual in the world today. America is the exception to all other countries. Our armed population has helped us win wars or at least avoid defeat. For example, a big reason why the Japanese never launched an invasion of the mainland US, even when we were at our most vulnerable after Pearl Harbor, was because they knew the people were armed. America's "hunters" represented the world's largest army.

In just one state, Pennsylvania, for example, just about a million hunting licenses are sold each year. I know that many non-hunters in Pennsylvania also have rifles, and pistols for self-protection.

So, how many guns are there in the US? According to the Geneva-based Small Arms Survey – the leading source of international public information about firearms – the U.S. has the best-armed civilian population in the world, with an estimated 270 million total guns. That's an average of 89 firearms for every 100 residents. It is far ahead of Yemen, which comes in second with about 55 firearms for every 100 people, or Switzerland, which is third with 46 guns for every 100 people.

The Founders did not spend a lot of time on documentation necessary to overthrow the government because they had a difficult time envisioning a scenario in which the recently freed people in the colonies, post revolution, would join an oppressive and tyrannical government, such as ours is today.

Where we are today, it assures that the worst of the worst get to decide which freedoms and liberties should remain with the people, and which ones an all knowing government should take away.

The Founders had created a set of rules, known as The Constitution to assure that all the people would be left with all freedom and all liberty in all cases. They did not want any scoundrels (politicians) messing with this notion or this nation.

Unfortunately, our legislators and at least one of our presidents in modern times have stopped full adherence to the Constitution and consequently, our freedom is now in jeopardy. Our representatives can stop this tonight or tomorrow or tomorrow night if they wish, the very next time Congress is in session. Ask them why they have not stopped the lawlessness already?

Americans must act at the voting booth

Unfortunately, last time I checked, the legislature (Congress in both Houses but mostly the US Senate) are more interested in being important in Washington than helping the folks back home. As we learn more about the Constitution, we may become brave enough to call them home and replace them with patriots from the ranks of normal citizens.

Only Americans, who hope to be in control of a communist state, advocate against the American way. Egalitarian principles of socialism simply mean that nobody gets to be part of the cream of the crop since the most equal spot for all is the bottom of the barrel.

Before this is fait accompli, Americans who love freedom have to do a little more than just speak up. We have to know what the founders would do to protect liberty and freedom and we simply have to do it or suffer the consequences. Reading this book is a good start. Thank you for taking the first step.

I do not have to preach freedom to 99% of Americans out there. We are all either products of good people who came here to be free or we came here ourselves to be free.

Permitting politicians from either party to talk us out of our birthright is not only dummm... it is asinine.

Yet, we can choose to be the dummmest Americans of all time or we can choose to engage, smarten up, stop being chumps, and take on these bad guys. They do not care at all about us.

Think of the leaders of the regimes that committed the atrocities that prompted our forefathers or us to come here. They were evil. They were bad. They would love to have their boot on your neck right now if you would let them.

I have had the pleasure of writing a lot of patriotic books. I write tech books and patriotic / political books. This is book # 53 of 66. It is really fun to help people with clear thinking.

Each time I write a book, I hope that I can attract another person into a love affair with America and its almost perfect Constitution. If you have read any of my other stuff, you know that I point out the bad guys and I pull no punches in my description of what we must do to escape from their reach. They will destroy us if we do not pay attention and escape their grasp.

Read the Federalist Papers

Before the patriotic "4 Dummmies" series, my last book was titled The Federalist Papers, by Hamilton, Jay, and Madison.

Since these eloquent founders had written the papers, my job was merely to arrange them in a 21st century orderly style and set them to print, I wrote no more than twenty pages of original introductory text to help persuade the potential reader that the rest of the Federalist Papers, for which they had paid was worth reading. I admit I did a bit more.

I took the patriotic essays of Alexander Hamilton, John Jay, and James Madison, known as The Federalist Papers, and I separated all of the two page and single page paragraphs, and half page paragraphs, and other large paragraphs, and I chopped them into smaller, more readable bits and pieces. Whether you buy a book or you download these essays free of charge, there is a lot of learning to be had in the Federalist Papers. But navigating the long paragraphs is a chore.

I literally had to wake myself up too many times in my initial reading of the Federalist Papers because they are tough to read in their natural form. Yet, they are very insightful. I know how tough it is to get through them as written in the original. I did not eliminate a word of the original. I just made it more readable. Check it out at www.bookhawkers.com.

By the way, just like The Constitution 4 Dummmies, My version of The Federalist Papers by Hamilton, Jay, And Madison also contains the full text of the US Constitution, The Declaration of Independence, The Articles of Confederation, The Bill of Rights, and lots of other good stuff that many of US over the years have forgotten.

Once you get back into these writings of the Founders, you will fully understand that they are the glue that keeps Americans free. They can help provide US all with liberty and freedom and justice forever and ever and ever… as long as we pay attention.

Having read the Federalist Papers myself, I feel like I should not be the one to offer this exhortation, but I shall anyway. If you can read every one of the Federalist Papers in the original, as offered on the Internet for free, you will have passed a great love test for America. And, if you do all the other things you need to do to be the citizen you would be proud to be, you then become worthy of the title, American.

Those of US, who read the Federalist Papers, though it is an arduous journey, know we have accomplished a lot. These papers—eighty-five articles written by Alexander Hamilton, John Jay, and James Madison, available for free on the Internet, quickly show US all that the founders were very concerned that the bad aspects of any other foreign government would not become part of the new American Democratic Republic. Today's administration in Washington and some others would give them pause for sure.

The founders were well aware of politicians and all of their negatives; but since they never put the notion of welfare, food stamps, and cell phones in the founding documents, they did not believe that the people would permit the Republic to be tainted by notions like socialism, progressivism, Marxism, or communism.

In the early days, the people were all aware of the sacrifices the early colonists had made to secure the new America. Never in the history of man was so much patriotism shown for a nation that might not ever make it into the future.

After enduring tyranny from England and other monarchies, Americans fought for and won the revolution against England et al for the cause of liberty and freedom. So that liberty and freedom would continue as long as possible and perhaps, forever, they built The Constitution.

Here we are 225 plus years later looking for hope and change rather than looking to the spirits of our founders to rebuild our fallen country. Hope will deliver nothing when action by well spirited citizens is required but discouraged.

I have found so many people, including myself, who at one time have forgotten the sacrifices of the revolutionaries and the gifts of freedom and liberty that were bestowed on all of US at the time of the revolutionary victory. All of these gifts have been emblazoned forever in our Constitution.

We Americans have been so blessed that we have not reminded ourselves enough over the years of our great heritage. Fourth of July celebrations are picnics, and though our parents have tried, the work of our founders and the great Constitution they built as the basis for all of our laws, is often lost in the celebration. Next boom you hear on the 4th, remember why and thank God for such brave men.

Neither freedom nor liberty come cheap so the next time an engaging politician offers you something for nothing, and in your heart, you know it is wrong; stick to your guns. Remember the words of Ben Franklin, a favorite US and Pennsylvania patriot:

"Those who desire to give up freedom in order to gain security will not have, nor do they deserve, either one." Amen!

Chapter 5

Throws the Bums Out!

Write opinion letters and call your representatives

The purpose of this book as noted from the beginning is to help US all be better Americans by understanding the Constitution along with America's founding. Most of us have seen or read or heard parts of the Constitution and if they have been presented properly, we more than likely, really like them.

The Constitution is the defining document of our country. It is the place to go to find out what America is all about! It is about the U.S. of A.—our nation. Our Country is what it is because its definition is embodied in the Constitution, which is America's most fundamental prized set of laws.

Our job, moving through life, of course is to learn what we can about our government (as defined by the Constitution). In this endeavor, we should all pay attention that our representatives actually spend their time representing US according to the laws of the founders.

When our representatives do not do the will of the people in-between elections we need to write letters to the editors of newspapers and other media, and write our Congressmen and Senators so they know they cannot snooker us.

If they don't listen, then we must do the honorable thing and write them even more letters, and letters to the editor and when they choose not to respond in our favor, we then can un-elect our leaders their next time out on the ballot.

Un-elect them! They would hate it!

Unfortunately for Americans, our representative in the Congress, the Supreme Court, and the Presidency is not Jefferson Smith from the movie Mr. Smith Goes to Washington. His honor is impeccable. But, the honor of our representatives is quite questionable.

Our representation has been getting progressively worse each year—not better. Over the past few years, since 2009 through 2016 especially with the healthcare debacle, it is clear that the voices of the people are not being heard in Washington, DC.

Just as Jefferson Smith in the Frank Capra classic movie, Mr. Smith Goes to Washington, found out, the corrupt purposes of elected officials is now in the open. It is to serve themselves by serving special interests.

In the sunlight of the day, therefore, the existing Congress— yes, both houses must go. Not the institution of Congress, just the corrupt members who choose not to serve the people.

We must bid them sayonara. We must say adieu. And when it comes time to elect our next President, and our next Congress; let's not forget to bring in an honest person who loves America as much as we do. If the mess we have today is not the president's intentions, and the president's direct fault, then whose fault, I might ask, is it? Might it be Stanley Laurel's or Oliver Hardy's—for it surely it is a comedy!!

Surprise in today's email

Before I get to this email, I got another surprise again today, while I am re-editing this book, hoping to clean it up for another printing. Before I show you the picture and the remarks I received, I was shopping at Malacari's, a great produce market in Wilkes-Barre PA today when I was joking around with the checkout person and the person behind me. I admitted that I was unemployed but I did not say I was writing books hoping the big ship would come in. Hah!

I said that I was thinking about running for President but it seemed that everybody was so happy with the current president that I figure I will have to look someplace else for employment. I then said that everybody loves him so much, I would not have a chance.

The cashier stopped in her tracks and said, that may have been a while ago but you should check again; it is not that way now. The lady behind her said that she did not think anybody liked him anymore. I have relatives in my family who are still doing well and they still love the president, so I figured the president was still doing OK. But, when these Jane Q Publics told me they were retired and collecting and still felt they had to work 'til they died, I started to think maybe you can't fool all of the people all of the time. It is encouraging that people are beginning to think.

In the same vein, another surprise from a famous artist and a magnificent painting that I show below.

This is the intro to this email before I show you the picture

Dear John,

I thought this an interesting fw – so true.

From: Trish
Sent: Saturday, June 07, 2014 9:39 AM
To: great people
Subject: RE: New Painting

If you are familiar with Jon McNaughton's paintings, you will love this one.

This is his latest---his opinions on the current situation are stated very clearly by his paintbrush and his comments below, but no comment is really needed.

McNaughton felt compelled to add text to his painting as follows:

Many Americans today feel a sense of dismay and horror as we see our country in a downward spiral; economically, morally, and politically. President Obama's indifferent attitude and the continuous list of scandals and bad policy are leading the country to ruin. As an artist I am reminded of the old saying "Nero fiddled while Rome burned." History believes that Nero himself may have set the great fire that burned a part of Rome during his leadership. Afterwards, he blamed it on the Christians who suffered great persecution under his rule. I see great similarities to what we are experiencing today. Obama fiddled, while the people witnessed the demise of America. **Jon McNaughton**

Again, it is not my intent to cast aspersions on the president. My purpose is to teach the Constitution to help all Americans know what to do to get from under the yoke of this president. The fact is that in this first section of the book, my intention is to build the case for the book. Why is this book necessary?

Look at McNaughton's painting and you get it clearly. America is falling apart and we want to save it. If President Obama is an innocent bystander then maybe someday, we can find a leader to help rescue us from his intransigence. Maybe!

The email explained immediately below is also reflective of today's major problems. If the president were to call me tonight after the book is released and ask me to remove all of the parts that are not favorable to him. I would do so immediately. I will replace those pages with my rationale for doing so. I don't expect a call, and that concerns me as an American, but at least I will have no additional work after this book is published.

Every now and then, we all get encouraged when somebody speaks out exactly how we all should be speaking out. As a conservative Democrat myself, trying to make this book apolitical, I thought about redacting parts of the note above and the email below that discuss people and party in specific terms. But, it is what it is.

I'll let the emails that I received speak for themselves and then after you read them both, we will move to the next section of this book. I once used this coming email in a book titled America 4 Dummmies, and I think it also fits US well here also, as we make our points in this book. Here it is:

Sent from my iPad

Begin forwarded message:
From: Roger
To: undisclosed-recipients:;
Subject: Fwd: FW: Two Americas

Two Americas

To add balance to the president's speech last night, read the below;

This is as well said as anything I have seen. Take the time to read it. No matter your political affiliation, Democrat, Republican, or Independent, it should be clear that this country is in a lot of trouble. Some of us will live long enough to see the consequences, but I really fear for our children and grandchildren's future. The damage that can and will be done over the next three years will likely be irreversible or take years to overcome.

In early January 2014, Bob Lonsberry, a Rochester talk radio personality on WHAM 1180 AM, said this in response to Obama's "income inequality speech":

To Americans

The Democrats are right, there are two Americas.

The America that works, and the America that doesn't. The America that contributes, and the America that doesn't. It's not the haves and the have not's, it's the do's and the don'ts. Some people do their duty as Americans, obey the law, support themselves, contribute to society, and others don't. That's the divide in America.

It's not about income inequality, it's about civic irresponsibility. It's about a political party that preaches hatred, greed and victimization in order to win elective office. It's about a political party that loves power more than it loves its country. That's not invective, that's truth, and it's about time someone said it.

The politics of envy was on proud display a couple weeks ago when President Obama pledged the rest of his term to fighting "income inequality." He noted that some people make more than other people that some people have higher incomes than others, and he says that's not just.

That is the rationale of thievery. The other guy has it, you want it, Obama will take it for you. Vote Democrat. That is the philosophy that produced Detroit. It is the electoral philosophy that is destroying America.

It conceals a fundamental deviation from American values and common sense because it ends up not benefiting the people who support it, but a betrayal. The Democrats have not empowered their followers; they have enslaved them in a culture of dependence and entitlement, of victimhood and anger instead of ability and hope.

The president's premise - that you reduce income inequality by debasing the successful - seeks to deny the successful the consequences of their choices and spare the unsuccessful the consequences of their choices.

Because, by and large, income variations in society is a result of different choices leading to different consequences. Those who choose wisely and responsibly have a far greater likelihood of success, while those who choose foolishly and irresponsibly have a far greater likelihood of failure. Success and failure usually manifest themselves in personal and family income.

You choose to drop out of high school or to skip college - and you are apt to have a different outcome than someone who gets a diploma and pushes on with purposeful education. You have your children out of wedlock and life is apt to take one course; you have them within a marriage and life is apt to take another course. Most often in life our destination is determined by the course we take.

My doctor, for example, makes far more than I do. There is significant income inequality between us. Our lives have had an inequality of outcome, but, our lives also have had an inequality of effort. While my doctor went to college and then devoted his young adulthood to medical school and residency, I got a job in a restaurant.

He made a choice, I made a choice, and our choices led us to different outcomes. His outcome pays a lot better than mine.

Does that mean he cheated and Barack Obama needs to take away his wealth? No, it means we are both free men in a free society where free choices lead to different outcomes.

It is not inequality Barack Obama intends to take away, it is freedom. The freedom to succeed, and the freedom to fail. There is no true option for success if there is no true option for failure.

The pursuit of happiness means a whole lot less when you face the punitive hand of government if your pursuit brings you more happiness than the other guy. Even if the other guy sat on his arse and did nothing. Even if the other guy made a lifetime's worth of asinine and shortsighted decisions.

Barack Obama and the Democrats preach equality of outcome as a right, while completely ignoring inequality of effort.

The simple Law of the Harvest - as ye sow, so shall ye reap - is sometimes applied as, "The harder you work, the more you get." Obama would turn that upside down. Those who achieve are to be punished as enemies of society and those who fail are to be rewarded as wards of society.

Entitlement will replace effort as the key to upward mobility in American society if Barack Obama gets his way. He seeks a lowest common denominator society in which the government besieges the successful and productive to foster equality through mediocrity.

He and his party speak of two Americas, and their grip on power is based on using the votes of one to sap the productivity of the other.

America is not divided by the differences in our outcomes, it is divided by the differences in our efforts. It is a false philosophy to say one man's success comes about unavoidably as the result of another man's victimization.

What Obama offered was not a solution, but a separatism. He fomented division and strife, pitted one set of Americans against another for his own political benefit. That's what socialists offer. Marxist class warfare wrapped up with a bow.

Two Americas, coming closer each day to proving the truth to Lincoln's maxim that a house divided against itself cannot stand. "

Wow! Isn't that why you are reading this book? Thank you Bob Lonsberry! We need more of you in our America!

Part II: The Fight for Independence

Chapter 6

From Colonialism to a Constitution

The Value of American History

This is not a book on American History as you well know by
now. It is a book about the Constitution and why the
Constitution helps all Americans, and why we must all protect
it from being torn apart by current politicians. It always helps
to get our patriotic juices flowing when we talk about how
brave the patriots were, who fought the war, and also those
behind the scenes that created the new government based on
the Constitution.

So, we go back in time a bit in a few short chapters to set the
stage for how we got our Constitution. It helps to know. I am
sure that many of us as brave as we may be, would have been
scared skinny to have had to participate in a bloody revolution
shortly after coming to a new world for freedom and liberty—
in order to keep your freedom and liberty.

This is the beginning of that story. Of course, today, our
liberty is being threatened by the very politicians we elect to
serve US. Not only should we be mad as hell, we should send
all these scalawag politicians back home and find some fine
Americans to take their places. It is never too late until it is
too late.

All Americans benefit from our democracy

Our Constitutional Representative Democracy, aka, our
Republic comes from the hard fought battles of the
Revolutionary War plus the craft of our Founders in writing
our country's original laws known as The Constitution.
Everything America was and is—is because of the work of the
great men who came before US.

Most Americans have a great feel for the notion of a
representative democracy and the sense that we elect
representatives of the community to handle our affairs in the
governing of our nation. We also have the privilege of a
Constitution which is intended to prevent tyranny by a
government gone wild. We do not have a direct democracy in
that we do not conduct the activities of government ourselves
in Washington. That is the job of our representatives. And
their job is to represent US.

It would be very difficult squeezing about 350 million people
into a room in Washington D.C. to vote on matters of country
in a direct democracy. Instead, we choose representatives
among US to get the job done. Is everything OK?

Something surely went wrong with the intention of
representation from the Founding Fathers to what
representation means today. Something went way wrong
sometime between 1492 and the present day but the evidence
suggests that the problem began closer to the year 2000 than
to the year 1400. That's not to say that all was hunky-dory in
the 1400s and onward. Humans are humans.

This is not a History book but it is a book about all of the
finest documents that were ever written by the Founders. The
major document in the history of America that has succeeded
in making America, America, is of course The Constitution of
the United States of America. We should all be thankful for
that.

Was it Columbus or Amerigo who discovered America?

When we learned about Columbus in grade school, we also learned a very small amount about America before 1492— before Columbus landed? We learned that our hemisphere had a very sparse population, and that the occupants were mostly nomadic tribes living off the wilderness. We also learned about some more developed cultures in Central and South America.

After all our learning, both pre-Columbus and post-Columbus, regardless of whether the ultimate discovery of America was made by Christopher Columbus, Amerigo Vespucci, Ponce de Leon, or Henry Cabot, America emerged as a strong entity. Historians are not 100% sure what came first but it is indisputable that they did not choose to call America, Columbia in honor of Columbus. Vespucci's first name was Amerigo, and so flows America.

Post Columbus, America saw the Jamestown Settlement bring in colonists, as well as the arrival of the Mayflower on continental US. Of course there are many stories about the First Thanksgiving, the Pilgrims, and the kind Indians who saved the pilgrims from extinction. Many books, including my own book, America 4 Dummmies tell those stories.

Conservative radio talk show host Rush Limbaugh threw his hat in the ring of patriotic founding books with a terrific, accurate, and interesting recounting of the Pilgrims and Thanksgiving. Limbaugh actually won Author of the Year award at the Children's Choice Book Awards for his book Rush Revere and the Brave Pilgrims: Time-Travel Adventures with Exceptional Americans.

In this book, a character who remarkably looks like Rush Limbaugh with a Patriot Hat and a wig, along with a talking horse named Liberty travel back in time to visit the pilgrims. It is a great book for kids and adults, and the audio version is also well done. Congratulations Rush! History is exciting!

Taking his pen out a second time for children, Limbaugh has another winner on his hands with Rush Revere and the First Patriots: Time-Travel Adventures with Exceptional Americans. Just as his first book, this story is both educational and entertaining!

In this book, Rush Revere, Liberty, the talking horse, and a couple of kids travel to events like the Boston Massacre, the Boston Tea Party, and even to Windsor Castle to meet with King George III. Among other things, life lessons can be learned including that "Freedom is from God. And when we fight for freedom we always fight on the side of God." Congratulations again Rush on a sure winner.

A few hundred years before the Revolution

The thirteen colonies of England were founded 100 + years after Columbus, with Virginia the first colony in 1607 and Georgia the last in 1733.

The individual colonies did not each have the same exact form of government but ultimately they all reported to the Crown of England. For example, one form of government was known as the Corporation. The colonies in this form were Massachusetts, Rhode Island, and Connecticut, though Rhode Island and Connecticut were also, "self-governing."

Besides the corporate form, there was also the provincial form of colony. The provincial forms included the proprietary colonies, Maryland, Pennsylvania, and Delaware, and the royal colonies, Virginia, North Carolina, South Carolina, New Hampshire, Vermont, New Jersey, and Georgia. There were thirteen in all at the Founding.

Most of these colonies, regardless of form, in early times had the same type of government consisting of a governor, appointed by the English Crown or by the proprietor(s). Additionally, they each had a council that also was appointed by the Crown. The most important body to the colonists was an assembly, which was known as the House of Representatives. In many ways, our country was formed to mimic the better parts of the Crown colonies.

The Governor

The Governor directly represented the Crown or the proprietor, who had already paid "allegiance" to the Crown with some type of tribute. Being the proprietor of a colony required a large stipend in cash or in kind.

The Council

Typically there were twelve men in the Council, though in Massachusetts there were twenty-eight. In Maryland, there were only three. Council members needed to possess certain attributes to retain their positions.

For example, they had to be residents of the colony in which they served, and they needed to be men of station and wealth. The Crown or the proprietor appointed the council so the normal conflicts arose and they were settled in the normal way -- in favor of the Crown or the proprietor. Council had three major functions:

- Advise the governor
- Provide the "upper house" of the legislature (Lords)
- Serve as the highest court in that particular colony

In Massachusetts, after 1691, the council was elected by a joint ballot of the legislature, called the General Court. In the other colonies it was by appointment of the Crown or the proprietors.

The House of Representatives

Then, there was the lower house which was elected by the people and whose mission in life was to represent and theoretically support the people. It was the body of the legislature that actually could tax the people.

To the victor belong the spoils

As the most successful imperialist nation of the day, Britain won control over American lands during the 17th and 18th centuries, and lost to the Americans in the late 18th century. Its control of the seas and its notion of colonial representative government were major factors in its ultimate success. The English nation of yore had a keen ability to recognize a good deal when it had one coming its way.

The European countries such as England, Holland (Dutch Republic), Spain, France, and Portugal developed colonies in the Western Hemisphere for many reasons, but primarily the reason was to bring in more revenue for the home state. England won all skirmishes and ultimately owned the colonies.

Though the English were late arrivals to America, they ultimately took all the spoils. The colonies were a great source of raw materials for trade (e.g. furs and precious metals) and they served as ready markets for finished products.

The Spanish, French, and Dutch had small settlements in what is now the continental US for a long time before the

English got fully involved. But, none of the settlements were of major consequence, and the English dominated.

As the thirteen colonies began to grow with immigrants pouring in from a number of different countries, these settlers, who more and more thought of themselves as Americans (what a nice thought), regardless of their origin, liked the English system of government much better than the authoritarian systems of the other countries.

Chapter 7

The Revolutionary War

The colonial love fest was over!

The beginning of the end of this love affair of the colonists with English-style government came about when the English government began to appear to the colonists as big bullies, and not grand protectors. The British began to impose direct controls and taxes on the colonial settlers. The French and Indian War had given England control of the thirteen colonies plus other American territories. They had yet to flex their muscles, but they were muscular indeed.

In the 1750's some historical estimates suggest that the 13 colonies had as many as 4 million people. King George III had concerns about how to protect so many people from invaders, be they American Indians or other European powers.

He chose to do so with a British army of 10,000 men stationed in America for the "protection of the colonists." Most colonists objected to a standing English army in the Americas, though many others had no issue with the idea. George III simply did not have the money for the protections he had agreed to provide, and he figured these "rich" colonists would be able to pay the freight. When the King decided the colonists should be taxed for their protection, things changed dramatically.

Stamp Act & the Intolerable Acts

England did not want to admit publicly that its resources had been stretched in all of the wars it had just won. The burden of providing the colonists with the protection they expected became a bit more than the British wanted to handle. But, they were not smart and they violated their own laws in order to collect taxes directly from the colonists. This made them no friends. England, the most powerful nation in the world chose not to ask the colonists. Instead, they decided to "take."

Without authority, for example, they simply imposed the Stamp Act of 1765. This tax was to be paid by having tax stamps placed on newspapers, licenses, calendars, playing cards, dice and other items that were frequently purchased in the colonies. Though the colonists' House of Representatives were empowered to bring matters of taxation forward, England had usurped their options. The colonists were surprised when England imposed taxes without American agreement or representation.

The Quartering Act

Another nasty little Act, which was imposed in 1765 along with the Stamp Act, then rescinded and brought back in 1774, was known as The Quartering Act. When brought back it was one of the four acts known as the Intolerable Acts, which were England's retaliation for the Boston TEA Party.

The second version in 1774 after a short repeal was also called the Quartering Act. Colonists despised this act. Instead of having to pay for the 1765 or 1774 equivalent of a hotel room, under this law, American colonists had to provide housing, candles, bedding, and beverages to the British soldiers stationed in the various colonies. Quartering means "Give them a room and amenities." American men and women were not very happy about giving up parts of their homes and their privacy to those they did not know.

Again the British were looking for a means to pay for their empire defense costs in America following the French and Indian War and another little war known as Pontiac's War.

In the same vein as the Stamp Act of this same year, this Act and various English Acts over time presented a big problem. After all, even the uninvolved without a dog in the fight can easily see that the whole thing was just an uninvited assertion of British authority over the colonies.

It completely disregarded the fact that troops had been financed for the prior 150 years by representative provincial assemblies (the colonists willingly) rather than by the Parliament and Crown in London. Americans wanted nothing to do with London controlling America—at least not so obviously and so forcefully.

Locations, which quartered more than their fair share of British soldiers, such as New York; resented the Quartering Act even more-so and they were outwardly defiant. The problem at this time was that there was no way that the British were about to go away empty handed.

They began to dig in more and more to protect their perceived "right" to get at the purse of the colonies through direct taxation, though in their own laws imposed for a long time on the colonists, they had excluded themselves from being legally able to coerce the colonists to pay or else. The colonists were incensed at the betrayal.

The British determination was felt as they exercised their strength in ways that the colonists had never before witnessed. Because of the resistance for example, of the first Quartering Act, for example, Britain almost immediately instituted the Suspending Act. But, their taxing ideas had not ceased.

This was insult to injury as it prohibited the New York Assembly from conducting any further business until the colony complied with the financial requirements of the resented Quartering Act. It was like England had declared war on New York.

When things did not look good, the British always seemed to do something to make matters worse.

For example, they also initiated another act that has been called the Townshend Act in which duties were imposed just as in the Stamp Act. This time the taxes were noted as Townsend duties and were applied to lead, glass, paper, and tea and the tax was payable immediately at colonial ports.

After a reprieve from the Quartering Act, in 1770, the colonists found themselves suffering from an additional quartering clause, which was included in the Intolerable Acts of 1774. The American Revolution was getting closer.

Americans were not ready for an imposition of such intolerable acts and the British were not ready to make America a loss-leader "possession." Parliament was not about to give up. They showed their resiliency to play another round by finding other means of taxing the colonists. Their next try was an import tax on everything. The colonists did more than offer objections.

Checkmate for the colonists when they boycotted all imports from England. After a few minor scuffles and 18 months of time, Parliament dropped the tax on everything but tea and then the British ships had to sail away from Boston Harbor.

In 1773, the British were back and at it again hoping that knowingly or unknowingly they could get the colonists to buy teas with the tax buried in the price. Shiploads of tea from India were of lower cost and they sold it so low that even with the tax included, many of the colonists, who enjoyed the English tea customs from the old world, could not resist purchasing it.

As most Americans well know the story, the Bostonians disguised themselves as Indians, snuck onto the ships and dumped about 340 tea chests into the sea. It was the Boston Tea Party and quite a party indeed.

Figure 10-1 Boston Tea Party

"The Destruction of Tea at Boston Harbor." 1773. Copy of lithograph by Sarony & Major, 1846. -- National Archives and Records Administration

This is another lesson in representative government. "No Taxation without Representation." And it certainly demonstrates how clever the constituency can become when made angry of taxes imposed by a body not representing the people. Shall we all take lessons?

In the past most Americans from grade school through high school learned the principles upon which this country was built and along with that the notion of representation.

The Intolerable Acts

The activity of the British known both as the "Intolerable Acts" and the "Coercive Acts," was so intolerable that it led to the colonists calling the first Continental Congress of the thirteen colonies. In other words, the USA, on its own, without even being the USA at the time, were getting ready to talk turkey long after the Pilgrims.

And, so, the colonies, knowing their representatives could be shot or otherwise held accountable by the British for treason of the Crown, chose to convene in Philadelphia's Carpenters Hall on September 5, 1774. Consider all of the delegates in this meeting as having begun the fight for your freedom.

Documents preceding the war

Two principal accomplishments of the Congress were the formation of a Continental Association as well as the Declaration of Rights and Grievances, a historical document included with explanation in this book.

The response to a potential revolution was in the offing as the colonists suspected. Brave as ever men would ever be, the colonists were ready to take on the Brits to preserve our America. That is why we celebrate the Fourth of July. Bravo to our patriots who fell in battle to preserve our freedom and liberty.

In preparation for a potential war with the Crown, the colonists began to train and gather arms and ammunition. They were brave indeed to take such action.

This preparation during the revolution made the American troops stronger in battle against the British professional army than even the British expected.

This was well noticed by British General Sir Thomas Gage, the Commander in Chief of the British forces and he became very concerned. Feeling that this was a plot of treason against the Crown, he planned to take action.

On the night of April 18, 1775, his troops seized some of the supplies and, according to some accounts; they planned to arrest two of the militia's leaders, Sam Adams and John Hancock.

Other accounts suggest that Gage didn't order troops to arrest John Hancock and Samuel Adams in Lexington on their way to Concord and as we have learned, such historian disputes almost never fully are resolved.

After Gage's papers were reflected in history, it is clear that a number of patriots thought that the capture of colonial leaders was probably the British column's mission, and they prepared accordingly. But, the facts indicate that was not really Gage's plan. Nonetheless, you can feel the type of tension that was growing between American patriots and the British army.

Paul Revere, an American hero for sure

Paul Revere had been a hero in the pre-revolution period in his ability to bring needed communication among the colonies about very important matters. Thanks to his warnings that the "British are coming," as well as those of William Dawes, Joseph Warren, and others, the militia was waiting for the British and thus the American Revolution began the next day.

Paul Revere and the other patriots rode from Boston to Concord, through the dark on the eve of April 19, 1775, to warn as many families and country folk as they could of the danger about to come.

The next day war broke out in the battles of Lexington and Concord. The revolution had begun. The unprepared and disorganized British ultimately had to retreat. The Minutemen prevailed and put the British on the chase. History will never forget that day.

Ralph Waldo Emerson, in his beloved Concord Hymn described the first shot fired by the patriots at the North Bridge as the "shot heard 'round the world." The clear irony of this shot however comes about because nobody knew then, nor is it known today; who it was who actually fired that first shot of the American Revolution.

It is as if from then 'til now, we moved from not being able to find a bullet, to not being able to find a huge Boeing 777 in the Indian Ocean. Who knows why? For the colonists, the mission was freedom, and the fact that a shot was fired, began the war. Whoever knows anything about the missing plane, I suspect will keep their silence. But if they were to speak either truth or fiction, there are those who believe that CNN would play it live.

No taxation without representation, the rationale for freedom, was a major cause of Americans joining in for the fight for liberty. Today, without bloodshed, the battle of the Whigs and the Tories continues in the halls of Congress while neither seems to care about the will of the people. You are reading this book because you care.

Unlike the late 1700's our new group of "representatives" does understand the value of public opinion and so these esteemed representatives in the U.S. in the latter part of the 20th century and past the first decade of the 21st seem much more ready to manipulate public opinion than to work to fulfill the public will.

Colonists in Boston had a lot of guts

Eventually, it got so bad in Boston that they threw crates of British Tea into Boston Harbor. The colonists were "mad as hell and were not going to take this anymore." As a reminder, in 1774, they held their First Continental Congress at Carpenter's Hall, Philadelphia to talk things over.

The colonists' resistance started peacefully with petitions and pamphlets and moved to intimidation, boycotts, and inter-colonial meetings. Many events as discussed above exacerbated the friction. These include the Boston Massacre, the Boston Tea Party, and the Coercive Acts. These destroyed the one-time good relations between Britain and its American colonies.

Attempts through the Sugar Act, the Stamp Act, and the Townshend Acts to raise money rather than simply control trade met with deep resistance in the colonies. Such taxation was something new. Parliament had previously passed measures to regulate trade in the colonies, but it had never before directly taxed the colonies to raise revenue

The severe tensions increased and the division escalated further after Parliament passed the Coercive Acts and so the First Continental Congress took the initial steps toward independence from Britain. Before the colonies gained real independence, however, they had begun to fight a long and bitter war. Historians know it as The Revolutionary War!

The patriots at the first Congress talked about plans to make Britain treat the colonies more fairly. Britain was the most powerful nation on earth at the time and it largely ignored these ideas and then sent its troops to control the colonists. The colonists had local militias at the time but chose to begin to recruit men from all of the states to handle this threat from England.

And, so the American Revolution began with the shot heard round the world in the battles of Lexington and Concord. In 1776, the colonists knew their world had become intolerable by the rapid British intrusion into American lives.

So, they wrote a number of declarations including the Declaration of Independence in which the US declared the American colonies were free from Britain's rule. At the same time, they kicked out the royal governors in the states and replaced them with American patriots.

The Declaration of Independence by Jefferson

Thomas Jefferson wrote most of the Declaration of Independence. The full Declaration with explanation is discussed in Chapter 11 and it is lightly referenced in Appendix C. It is surely inspiring: Thomas Paine, a great patriot wrote this short piece called Crisis about the events to come:

The Crisis
by Thomas Paine, December 23, 1776

"THESE are the times that try men's souls. The summer soldier and the sunshine patriot will, in this crisis, shrink from the service of their country; but he that stands by it now, deserves the love and thanks of man and woman. Tyranny, like hell, is not easily conquered; yet we have this consolation with us, that the harder the conflict, the more glorious the triumph. What we obtain too cheap, we esteem too lightly: it is dearness only that gives every thing its value. Heaven knows how to put a proper price upon its goods; and it would be strange indeed if so celestial an article as FREEDOM should not be highly rated. Britain, with an army to enforce her tyranny, has declared that she has a right (not only to TAX) but "to BIND us in ALL CASES WHATSOEVER" and if being bound in that manner, is not slavery, then is there not such a thing as slavery upon earth. Even the expression is impious; for so unlimited a power can belong only to God...."

Chapter 8

About the Revolutionary War

Britain was determined to lose

The British had many advantages in the war, such as a trained Army and Navy. They also had many loyalists among the colonists who instead of supporting the revolution, supported the British Empire.

Colonists at the time from North and South had been accustomed to view slaves as property and among other things, they did not like the notion proposed by Lord Dunmore to free slaves who joined the Royal Army.

Independent of the slavery issue, the patriots were inspired by Thomas Paine's pamphlet called Common Sense. In clear, simple language this short literary work explained the advantages of and the need for immediate independence. You may read this work by Paine for free: http://www.ushistory.org/PAINE/commonsense/singlehtml .htm

As we all know, American colonists known as patriots won the war for all of US. Most historians credit the bravery and willingness to risk it all of the colonists, the excellent leadership of George Washington; the aid of such European nations as France; and the many tactical errors by British commanders as the significant factors that contributed to the American victory.

The British strategy called for crushing the rebellion in the North first and they almost succeeded but for the bravery of the patriots. Several times the British nearly defeated the Continental Army. This took its toll on the morale of the American fighters.

Major victories at Trenton and Princeton, N.J., in late 1776 and early 1777 restored patriot hopes, and then another victory at Saratoga, N.Y. halted a major British advance from Canada, and eventually France, certainly not a friend of England's at the time, and looking for its own opportunities in the New World, intervened on behalf of the Patriots and contributed very positively to the win.

Then, in 1778, fighting moved to the South and again Britain was successful. They captured Georgia and Charleston, S.C. and defeated an American army at Camden, S.C. However, as things were getting dire, a band of patriots began to harass loyalists and they disrupted the supply lines.

Thus, Britain failed to achieve control over the southern countryside before they were compelled to advance northward to Yorktown, Va. In the war's last major battle, in 1781, an American and French force defeated the British at Yorktown. It was all over but the agreements for peace.

At the time of the Revolution, there were about four or five million colonists in the New World. Not all were patriots of course. The peace came with a high price. Some of the unintended consequences of the war include the following:

About 7,200 Americans died during the battles of the Revolution. Another 10,000 died fighting the elements suffering from disease or exposure. Another 8,500 or so died in British prisons.

At least a quarter of the slaves in South Carolina and Georgia freed themselves during the Revolution. The Northern states chose to outlaw slavery outright or they adopted gradual emancipation plans.

The states were no longer under British control and so they each adopted written constitutions guaranteeing freedom of speech and religious freedom. They also increased the legislature's size and powers, made taxation more progressive, and reformed inheritance laws.

Cornwallis Surrenders marking the end of the Revolutionary War

George Washington was by many accounts the most competent and the bravest American hero of all times, though he was not killed in action. This future president made significant progress prosecuting the War of Independence.

When the Continental Army arrived in Yorktown on September 26, 1783, near the end of the war, the French Fleet, was in firm control of the bay. The French, operating under the Franco-American Alliance, had offered substantial assistance to the new United Sates.

They had Britian's Cornwallis pinned in. With about 20,000 troops from state militias combined with troops from France, the American forces had stymied the British who were being led by General Lord Charles Cornwallis. Cornwallis's troops were taking heavy casualties from a constant bombardment.

Cornwallis was the 2nd General in Command in the Americas, and to put it frankly, when reinforcements from New York, sent by Britain's Top General Henry Clinton, did not arrive in time to be of use, he knew he was licked and so he surrendered on October 19, 1781. This was the de-facto end of the war though skirmishes continued for several years.

Figure 4-4 Surrender of Cornwallis

Surrender Of Cornwallis - The End of the American Revolution.

In December 1783, George Washington made the end of the American Revolution official when he resigned his commission to Congress. The revolution had ended. America had achieved its independence and its representative democracy was about to get even stronger.

It was time to write down the principles of this new nation. In the next section, we show the original text of the historic documents showing American principles. Following significant original document text, your author provides explanatory text in each document so that all Americans can understand the meaning of the Founders' precepts.

When we get to the Constitution, you will see that a great deal of explanatory text is used to explain the various Articles and Sections. Hold on to your seats folks, the document ride is about to begin:

Part III Patriotic Documents Before the Constitution

Chapter 9

The Declaration of Rights and Grievances

Representation at All Levels

One of the first documents on the way to the *Declaration of Independence* and *The Constitution* was the *Declaration of Rights and Grievances,* It was a product of the First Continental Congress. The colonists were upset with foreign rule from England because they were not given a real voice in the government. As an aside, unfortunately not much has changed for regular American citizens since that time.

The First Document on the way to the American Revolution

As shown in its entirety below, the *Declaration of Rights and Grievances* was the first formal request of the "United States" to England for a return to representative government, in the form as had originally been established by the Crown.
Though nothing close to a constitutional democracy, the Colonists under English rule enjoyed representation in the lower house of the colonial governments.

There was no union of colonies or states at the time and had the English kept to themselves and not levied taxes directly on the colonists, Americans today would be much more interested if Camilla is really ever going to be the Queen.

With a careful reading of the Declaration of Rights and Grievances, one can get a quick sense of what the colonists wanted from the Crown. It was simply, "no taxation without representation," and all of the many positions this plea represented. As the thought of a revolution became more of a reality for the Patriots, independence and freedom and liberty became even more important than the tax burden.

This early declaration was the first major document of the new government of the United States, though it occurred at a time when the states were not actively seeking independence from the Crown.

The expressed purpose of the First Continental Congress held in 1774 was:

"That a Committee be appointed to state the rights of the Colonies in general, the several instances in which these rights are violated or infringed, and the means most proper to be pursued for obtaining a restoration of them."

The committee was constructed and the declaration was drafted and it was read on September 22nd and the draft of the grievances was read on the 24th. The members of the First Congress debated the drafts on October 12 and 13, and after a final draft was produced, it was agreed on Friday, October 14, 1774.

At this First Continental Congress, the delegates drafted several documents, and several drafts of documents, one of which was the document known as The Declaration of Rights and Grievances. This was the statement of American complaints agreed to on October 14, 1774. It was sent to King George III, to whom, at the time, many of the delegates remained loyal. It was not sent to Parliament since the delegates did not have the same level of loyalty to this body. Quite frankly, the document implored King George III to step in and rescue the colonies from the English Parliament.

The radical colonial delegates were critical of this particular Declaration because it continued to concede the right of Parliament to regulate colonial trade, a view that was losing favor in the mid-1770s. Many suggest that the actual cause of the American Revolution is found in this major historical document.

The document follows on the next page:

Thus, In the First Continental Congress, which met in September and October 1774, the delegates of the Congress made several major decisions. Among those was to send King George III this Declaration of Rights and Grievances, which is shown below:.

[I trust you will find that much of this document is very readable and does not need additional comment or explanation. In each of the Resolves, we have added an explanation to help in understanding its meaning and importance.]

In Congress, at Philadelphia, October 14, 1774

Whereas, since the close of the last war, the British Parliament, claiming a power of right to bind the people of America, by statute, all cases whatsoever, hath in some acts expressly imposed taxes on them and in others, under various pretenses, but in fact for the purpose raising a revenue, hath imposed rates and duties payable in these colonies established a board of commissioners, with unconstitutional powers, and extended the jurisdiction of courts of admiralty, not only for collecting the said duties, but for the trial of causes merely arising within the body of a county. And whereas, in consequence of other statutes, judges, who before held only estates at will in their offices, have been made dependent on the Crown alone for their salaries, and standing armies kept in time of peace:

And whereas, it has lately been resolved in Parliament, that by force of a statute, made in the thirty-fifth year of the reign of Henry the Eighth, colonists may be transported to England, and tried there upon accusations for treasons, and misprisions, or concealments of treasons committed in the colonies, and by a late statute, such trials have been directed in cases therein mentioned.

And whereas, in the last session of Parliament, three statutes were made; one, entitled "An act to discontinue, in such manner and for such time as are therein mentioned, the landing and discharging, lading, or shipping of goods, wares and merchandise, at the town, and within the harbor of Boston, in the province of Massachusetts Bay, in North America"; and another, entitled "An act for the better regulating the government of the province of the Massachusetts Bay in New England"; and another, entitled "An act for the impartial administration of justice, in the cases of persons questioned for any act done by them in the execution of the law, or for the suppression of riots and tumults in the province of the Massachusetts Bay, in New England." And another statute was then made, "for making more effectual provision for the government of the province of Quebec, etc." All which statutes are impolitic, unjust and cruel, as well as unconstitutional, and most dangerous and destructive of American rights.

And whereas, assemblies have been frequently dissolved, contrary to the rights of the people, when they attempted to deliberate on grievances; and their dutiful, humble, loyal, and reasonable petitions to the Crown for redress, have been repeatedly treated with contempt by His Majesty's ministers of state:

The good people of the several colonies of New Hampshire, Massachusetts Bay, Rhode Island and Providence Plantations, Connecticut, New York, New Jersey, Pennsylvania, New Castle, Kent and Sussex on Delaware, Maryland, Virginia, North Carolina, and South Carolina, justly alarmed at these arbitrary proceedings of Parliament and administration, have severally elected, constituted, and appointed deputies to meet and sit in general congress, in the city of Philadelphia, in order to obtain such establishment, as that their religion, laws, and liberties may not be subverted.

Whereupon the deputies so appointed being now assembled, in a full and free representation of these colonies, taking into their most serious consideration, the best means of attaining the ends aforesaid, do, in the first place, as Englishmen, their ancestors in like cases have usually done, for asserting and vindicating their rights and liberties, declare,

That the inhabitants of the English colonies in North America, by the immutable laws of nature, the principles of the English Constitution, and the several charters or compacts, have the following rights:

Resolved, N.C.D. 1. *That they are entitled to life, liberty, and property, and they have never ceded to any sovereign power whatever, a right to dispose of either without their consent.*

Resolved, N.C D. 2. *That our ancestors, who first settled these colonies, were at the time of their emigration from the mother country, entitled to all the rights, liberties, and immunities of free and natural-born subjects, within the realm of England.*

Resolved, N.C.D. 3. *That by such emigration they by no means forfeited, surrendered, or lost any of those rights, but that they were, and their descendants now are, entitled to the exercise and enjoyment of all such of them, as their local and other circumstances enable them, to exercise and enjoy.*

[Explanation of Resolves 1 to 3: These resolves mean that upon emigration from Great Britain, the colonists were entitled to equal rights as the British, and should be treated as such. This is in reference to the Intolerable Acts that the colonists saw as limiting their freedom and placing them at a lower political and social level than the citizens of the mother country. This resolve is controversial as it suggests that colonial rights have not only been disrespected recently prior to the Continental Congress, but rather for many years before.]

Resolved, N.C.D 4. *That the foundation of English liberty, and of all free government, is a right in the people to* *participate in their legislative council: and as the English colonists are not represented, and from their local and other circumstances, cannot properly be represented in the British Parliament, they are entitled to a free and exclusive power of legislation in their several provincial legislatures, where their right of representation can alone be preserved, in all cases of taxation and internal polity, subject only to the negative of their sovereign, in such manner as has been heretofore used and accustomed. But, from the necessity of the case, and a regard to the mutual interest of both countries, we cheerfully consent to the operation of such acts of the British Parliament, as are bona fide, restrained to the regulation of our external commerce, for the purpose of securing the commercial advantages of the whole empire to the mother country, and the commercial benefits of its respective members; excluding every idea of taxation, internal or external, for raising a revenue on the subjects in America, without their consent.*

[Explanation of Resolve 4: The colonies were under British Control in 1774. Colonists did not have the direct representation in the British Parliament, as those living in England. Because of stipulations in the British Constitution, the colonists believed that the government couldn't place taxes on them unless they had representatives in the government. The colonists did not want to have taxes levied on them to raise money for the British government when they had no say in the legislature of such taxes. In reality, the British were implementing these taxes to raise the revenue they lost in the <u>French and Indian War</u>, as well as to will the colonies into submission at a time when the British felt their loyalty was wavering. The colonists' slogan for this issue was "<u>No taxation without representation.</u>"]

Resolved, N.C.D. 5. *That the respective colonies are entitled to the common law of England, and more especially to the great and inestimable privilege of being*

*tried by their peers of the vicinage, according to the course
of that law.*

[Explanation of Resolve 5: In the Administration of Justice
Act it was made law that the colonists had to be tried in
British courts for crimes, and British soldiers accused of
crimes in America could also be tried in British courts. The
colonists saw this as unfair and called this the "murder act."
They believed that soldiers could get away with murder by
fleeing when they were supposed to go to Britain for trial. In
essence the colonists were demanding that they be tried in
their own courts for crimes committed in the colonies.**]**

Resolved, N.C.D. 6. *That they are entitled to the benefit of
such of the English statutes as existed at the time of their
colonization; and which they have, by experience,
respectively found to be applicable to their several local
and other circumstances.*

Resolved, N.C.D. 7. *That these, His Majesty's colonies,
are likewise entitled to all the immunities and privileges
granted and confirmed to them by royal charters, or
secured by their several codes of provincial laws.*

[Explanation of Resolves 6 & 7: These resolves demand
that the colonists are entitled to the rights stated in their
individual colony's charters, as existed since colonization.
This also was a pillar upon which colonial rights rested, in
comparison to the rights of the monarch over the colonies.
The colonial charter must be respected.**]**

Resolved, N.C.D. 8. *That they have a right peaceably to
assemble, consider of their grievances, and petition the
King; and that all prosecutions, prohibitory proclamations,
and commitment for the same, are illegal.*

[Explanation of Resolve 8: Hoping to ease the tension the
colonies needed to make sure they had the right to
assemble and petition the king, in the forms of both
legitimate <u>committees of correspondence</u>. These types of

committees were formed in the period between 1772 and 1774 as a way for colonists and colonial leaders to express their grievances towards the King. Nobody among the colonists wanted such rights to go away.]

Resolved, N.C.D. 9. *That the keeping a standing army in these colonies, in times of peace, without the consent of the legislature of that colony, in which such army is kept, is against law.*

[Explanation of Resolve 9: Colonists were enraged that British soldiers were authorized by the crown to room and board at any colonists home they chose. The British had placed a permanent army in Massachusetts in 1768, and this too brought the ire of the colonists as the troops needed quartering and the colonists did not want combat brigades at their front doors. As noted, the colonists were angered that these troops were to be quartered in their houses, fed with their food, and they saw it as a manifestation of the blatant mistrust from Britain in exacting even greater control in the colonies.]

Resolved, N.C.D. 10. *It is indispensably necessary to good government, and rendered essential by the English constitution, that the constituent branches of the legislature be independent of each other; that, therefore, the exercise of legislative power in several colonies, by a council appointed, during pleasure by the Crown, is unconstitutional, dangerous, and destructive to the freedom of American legislation.*

All and each of which the aforesaid deputies, in behalf of themselves and their constituents, do claim, demand, and insist on, as their indubitable rights and liberties; which cannot be legally taken from them, altered or abridged by any power whatever, without their own consent, by their representatives in their several provincial legislatures.

In the course of our inquiry, we find many infringements and violations of the foregoing rights, which, from an ardent desire, that harmony and mutual intercourse of affection and interest may be restored, we pass over for the present, and proceed to state such acts and measures as have been adopted since the last war, which demonstrate a system formed to enslave America.

[**Explanation of Resolve 10:** The colonists were not interested in becoming slaves of Britain. They resented being controlled by a council appointed by the British Crown, and demanded their council be from the colonists and leaders of their own choosing. The addition of this resolve shows that the colonists were demanding a level of colonial independence and were not interested in attempts by Britain to control the colonies with an iron fist. However, the colonist recognized the power of the Crown.]

[In the next set of unnumbered Resolves, they get a bit more specific as to the items they find as violations of a trusting relationship between the Crown and the colonies.]

Resolved, N.C.D. *That the following acts of Parliament are infringements and violations of the rights of the colonists; and that the repeal of them is essentially necessary in order to restore harmony between Great Britain and the American colonies, viz;*

The several acts of 4 Geo. 3. ch. 15, and ch. 34.--5 Geo. 3. ch. 25.--6 Geo. 3. ch. 52.--7 Geo. 3. ch. 41, and ch. 46.--8 Geo. 3. ch. 22, which impose duties for the purpose of raising a revenue in America, extend the powers of the admiralty court beyond their ancient limits, deprive the American subject of trial by jury, authorize the judges' certificate to indemnify the prosecutor from damages, that he might otherwise be liable to, requiring oppressive security from a claimant of ships and goods seized, before he shall be allowed to defend his property, and are subversive of American rights.

Also the 12 Geo. 3. ch. 24, entitled "An act for the better securing His Majesty's dock yards, magazines, ships, ammunition, and stores," which declares a new offense in America, and deprives the American subject of a constitutional trial by jury of the vicinage, by authorizing the trial of any person, charged with the committing any offense described in the said act, out of the realm, to be indicted and tried for the same in any shire or county within the realm.

Also the three acts passed in the last session of Parliament, for stopping the port and blocking up the harbor of Boston, for altering the charter and government of the Massachusetts Bay, and that which is entitled "An act for the better administration of justice," etc.

Also the act passed in the same session for establishing the Roman Catholic religion in the province of Quebec, abolishing the equitable system of English laws, and erecting a tyranny there, to the great danger, from so total a dissimilarity of religion, law, and government of the neighboring British colonies, by the assistance of whose blood and treasure the said country was conquered from France.

Also the act passed in the same session for the better providing suitable quarters for officers and soldiers in His Majesty's service in North America.

Also, that the keeping a standing army in several of these colonies, in time of peace, without the consent of the legislature of that colony in which such army is kept, is against law.

To these grievous acts and measures, Americans cannot submit, but in hopes that their fellow subjects in Great Britain will, on a revision of them, restore us to that state in which both countries found happiness and prosperity, we have for the present only resolved to pursue the following peaceable measures:

1. To enter into a non-importation, non-consumption, and non-exportation agreement or association.

2. To prepare an address to the people of Great Britain, and a memorial to the inhabitants of British America, and

3. To prepare a loyal address to His Majesty; agreeable to resolutions already entered into.

And so the final resolve in this document refers to all of the intolerable acts of Great Britain against the colonists, and it avers that under the Declaration and Resolves of the First Continental Congress, they are prohibited and illegal.

American anger over the Intolerable Acts was no secret to the British government, and the issue of taxation without representation was voiced loudly. However, this resolve does question the authority of the monarch and parliaments rule in the colonies, and so it was sent with some level of trepidation for the colonists were not looking, at this time for a big war…but they were not looking for a peace that stole their freedoms, either.

Chapter 10

The Articles of Association Part I

Another Act of the First Continental Congress!

Several days after the signing and sending of the Declaration of Rights and Grievances to England, on October 20, 1774, the Congress passed the Articles of Association. They had been written during the same Congress. The Congress, by the way was the colonial Congress (First Continental Congress) and not the Congress of today, with a House and a Senate as created by The Constitution. The Constitution was about fifteen years away at this time in history.

The Articles of Association were also addressed to King George III. In essence, it was a formal agreement of the colonies themselves to work together as an association of states with common purpose. How King George would react to such demands was an interesting consideration. The colonist patriots were extremely brave men.

It was basically a union of protest and boycott as many of the articles outlined the specifications that the colonists were to take regarding the export and import of goods.

As you read these articles below, also lightly referenced in Appendix B, you can't help but notice the elegance and forethought in the draft. We are a fortunate lot indeed to have had such fine and capable, and yes, honorable men, representing America in our founding days.

Both the Declaration of Rights and Grievances as shown in the prior chapter as well as the Articles of Association shown below were prompted substantially by the Coercive Acts of Parliament enacted in the 1774 time frame.

The Coercive Acts by Parliament included the following:

1. The Boston Port Act closed the port of Boston until damages from the Boston Tea Party were paid.

2. The Massachusetts Government Act restricted Massachusetts; democratic town meetings and turned the governor's council into an appointed body.

3. The Administration of Justice Act made British officials immune to criminal prosecution in Massachusetts.

4. The Quartering Act revisited from 1765, required colonists to house and quarter British troops on demand, including in their private homes as a last resort.

5. The Quebec Act. Though not technically part of the Coercive Acts, the colonists lumped a fifth act, known as the Quebec Act along with the four Coercive acts into a set of five that they referred to as "The Intolerable Acts." The Quebec Act extended freedom of worship to Catholics in Canada, as well as granting Canadians the continuation of their judicial system. Religious tolerance at the time was not at its best. The mainly Protestant colonists did not look kindly on the ability of Catholics to worship freely on their borders.

Let's now take a look at the Articles of Association as another major document that helps define the American thought process before America was ready to take up arms against England. Because sometimes the long paragraphs of the founders, though quite eloquent, put my contemporaries to sleep. I have parsed some material in the Articles of Association to be more readable without removing any words.

The Articles of Association are given below. In Part II of Chapter 10, the articles are explained in English.

The Articles of Association

October 20, 1774

We, his majesty's most loyal subjects, the delegates of the several colonies of New-Hampshire, Massachusetts-Bay, Rhode-Island, Connecticut, New-York, New-Jersey, Pennsylvania, the three lower counties of Newcastle, Kent and Sussex on Delaware, Maryland, Virginia, North-Carolina, and South-Carolina, deputed to represent them in a continental Congress, held in the city of Philadelphia, on the 5th day of September, 1774, avowing our allegiance to his majesty, our affection and regard for our fellow-subjects in Great-Britain and elsewhere, affected with the deepest anxiety, and most alarming apprehensions, at those grievances and distresses, with which his Majesty's American subjects are oppressed; and having taken under our most serious deliberation, the state of the whole continent, find, that the present unhappy situation of our affairs is occasioned by a ruinous system of colony administration.

[Such Administration] was adopted by the British ministry about the year 1763, evidently calculated for enslaving these colonies, and, with them, the British Empire. In prosecution of which system, various acts of parliament have been passed, for raising a revenue in America, for depriving the American subjects, in many instances, of the constitutional trial by jury, exposing their lives to danger, by directing a new and illegal trial beyond the seas, for crimes alleged to have been committed in America:

And in prosecution of the same system, several late, cruel, and oppressive acts have been passed, respecting the town of Boston and the Massachusetts-Bay, and also an act for extending the province of Quebec, so as to border on the western frontiers of these colonies, establishing an arbitrary government therein, and discouraging the settlement of British subjects in that wide extended country.

Thus, by the influence of civil principles and ancient prejudices, to dispose the inhabitants to act with hostility against the free Protestant colonies, whenever a wicked ministry shall choose so to direct them.

To obtain redress of these grievances, which threaten destruction to the lives liberty, and property of his majesty's subjects, in North-America, we are of opinion, that a non-importation, non-consumption, and non-exportation agreement, faithfully adhered to, will prove the most speedy, effectual, and peaceable measure.

And, therefore, we do, for ourselves, and the inhabitants of the several colonies, whom we represent, firmly agree and associate, under the sacred ties of virtue, honour and love of our country, as follows:

1. That from and after the first day of December next, we will not import, into British America, from Great-Britain or Ireland, any goods, wares, or merchandise whatsoever, or from any other place, any such goods, wares, or merchandise, as shall have been exported from Great-Britain or Ireland; nor will we, after that day, import any East-India tea from any part of the world; nor any molasses, syrups, paneles, coffee, or pimento, from the British plantations or from Dominica; nor wines from Madeira, or the Western Islands; nor foreign indigo.

2. We will neither import nor purchase, any slave imported after the first day of December next; after which time, we will wholly discontinue the slave trade, and will neither be concerned in it ourselves, nor will we hire our vessels, nor sell our commodities or manufactures to those who are concerned in it.

3. As a non-consumption agreement, strictly adhered to, will be an effectual security for the observation of the non-importation, we, as above, solemnly agree and associate, that from this day, we will not purchase or use any tea, imported on account of the East-India company, or any on which a duty bath been or shall be paid; and from and after the first day of March next, we will not purchase or use any East-India tea whatever; nor will we, nor shall any person for or under us, purchase or use any of those goods, wares, or merchandise, we have agreed not to import, which we shall know, or have cause to suspect, were imported after the first day of December, except such as come under the rules and directions of the tenth article hereafter mentioned.

4. The earnest desire we have not to injure our fellow-subjects in Great-Britain, Ireland, or the West-Indies, induces us to suspend a non-exportation, until the tenth day of September, 1775; at which time, if the said acts and parts of acts of the British parliament herein after mentioned, are not repealed, we will not directly or indirectly, export any merchandise or commodity whatsoever to Great-Britain, Ireland, or the West-Indies, except rice to Europe.

5. Such as are merchants, and use the British and Irish trade, will give orders, as soon as possible, to their factors, agents and correspondents, in Great-Britain and Ireland, not to ship any goods to them, on any pretence whatsoever, as they cannot be received in America; and if any merchant, residing in Great-Britain or Ireland, shall directly or indirectly ship any goods, wares or merchandize, for America, in order to break the said non-importation agreement, or in any manner contravene the same, on such unworthy conduct being well attested, it ought to be made public; and, on the same being so done, we will not, from thenceforth, have any commercial connection with such merchant.

6. That such as are owners of vessels will give positive orders to their captains, or masters, not to receive on board their vessels any goods prohibited by the said non-importation agreement, on pain of immediate dismission from their service.

7. We will use our utmost endeavors to improve the breed of sheep, and increase their number to the greatest extent; and to that end, we will kill them as seldom as may be, especially those of the most profitable kind; nor will we export any to the West-Indies or elsewhere; and those of us, who are or may become overstocked with, or can conveniently spare any sheep, will dispose of them to our neighbors, especially to the poorer sort, on moderate terms.

8. We will, in our several stations, encourage frugality, economy, and industry, and promote agriculture, arts and the manufactures of this country, especially that of wool; and will discountenance and discourage every species of extravagance and dissipation, especially all horse-racing, and all kinds of games, cock fighting, exhibitions of shows, plays, and other expensive diversions and entertainments; and on the death of any relation or friend, none of us, or any of our families will go into any further mourning-dress, than a black crepe or ribbon on the arm or hat, for gentlemen, and a black ribbon and necklace for ladies, and we will discontinue the giving of gloves and scarves at funerals.

9. Such as are venders of goods or merchandize will not take advantage of the scarcity of goods, that may be occasioned by this association, but will sell the same at the rates we have been respectively accustomed to do, for twelve months last past. -And if any vender of goods or

merchandise shall sell such goods on higher terms, or shall, in any manner, or by any device whatsoever, violate or depart from this agreement, no person ought, nor will any of us deal with any such person, or his or her factor or agent, at any time thereafter, for any commodity whatever.

10. In case any merchant, trader, or other person, shall import any goods or merchandize, after the first day of December, and before the first day of February next, the same ought forthwith, at the election of the owner, to be either re-shipped or delivered up to the committee of the country or town, wherein they shall be imported, to be stored at the risk of the importer, until the non-importation agreement shall cease, or be sold under the direction of the committee aforesaid; and in the last-mentioned case, the owner or owners of such goods shall be reimbursed out of the sales, the first cost and charges, the profit, if any, to be applied towards relieving and employing such poor inhabitants of the town of Boston, as are immediate sufferers by the Boston port-bill; and a particular account of all goods so returned, stored, or sold, to be inserted in the public papers; and if any goods or merchandizes shall be imported after the said first day of February, the same ought forthwith to be sent back again, without breaking any of the packages thereof.

11. That a committee be chosen in every county, city, and town, by those who are qualified to vote for representatives in the legislature, whose business it shall be attentively to observe the conduct of all persons touching this association; and when it shall be made to appear, to the satisfaction of a majority of any such committee, that any person within the limits of their appointment has violated this association, that such majority do forthwith cause the truth of the case to be published in the gazette; to the end, that all such foes to the rights of British-America may be publicly known, and universally contemned as the enemies of American liberty; and thenceforth we respectively will break off all dealings with him or her.

12. That the committee of correspondence, in the respective colonies, do frequently inspect the entries of their customhouses, and inform each other, from time to time, of the true state thereof, and of every other material circumstance that may occur relative to this association.

13. That all manufactures of this country be sold at reasonable prices, so- that no undue advantage be taken of a future scarcity of goods.

14. And we do further agree and resolve that we will have no trade, commerce, dealings or intercourse whatsoever, with any colony or province, in North-America, which shall not accede to, or which shall hereafter violate this association, but will hold them as unworthy of the rights of freemen, and as inimical to the liberties of their country.

And we do solemnly bind ourselves and our constituents, under the ties aforesaid, to adhere to this association, until such parts of the several acts of parliament passed since the close of the last war, as impose or continue duties on tea, wine, molasses, syrups, paneles, coffee, sugar, pimento, indigo, foreign paper, glass, and painters' colors, imported into America, and extend the powers of the admiralty courts beyond their ancient limits, deprive the American subject of trial by jury, authorize the judge's certificate to indemnify the prosecutor from damages, that he might otherwise be liable to from a trial by his peers, require oppressive security from a claimant of ships or goods seized, before he shall be allowed to defend his property, are repealed.

-And until that part of the act of the 12 G. 3. ch. 24, entitled "An act for the better securing his majesty's dock-yards magazines, ships, ammunition, and stores," by which any persons charged with committing any of the offenses therein described, in America, may be tried in any shire or county within the realm, is repealed-and until the four acts, passed the last session of parliament, viz. that for stopping the port and blocking up the harbor of Boston-that for altering the charter and government of the Massachusetts-

Bay-and that which is entitled "An act for the better administration of justice, &c."-and that "for extending the limits of Quebec, &c." are repealed.

And we recommend it to the provincial conventions, and to the committees in the respective colonies, to establish such farther regulations as they may think proper, for carrying into execution this association.

The foregoing association being determined upon by the Congress, was ordered to be subscribed by the several members thereof; and thereupon, we have hereunto set our respective names accordingly.

IN CONGRESS, PHILADELPHIA, October 20, 1774.
PEYTON RANDOLPH, President.

New Hampshire -- *John Sullivan, Nathaniel Folsom*

Massachusetts Bay -- *Thomas Cushing, Samuel Adams, John Adams, Robert Treat Paine*

Rhode Island -- *Stephen Hopkins, Samuel Ward*

Connecticut -- *Eliphalet Dyer, Roger Sherman, Silas Deane*

New York -- *Isaac Low, John Alsop, John Jay, James Duane, Philip Livingston, William Floyd, Henry Wisner, Simon. Boerum*

New Jersey -- *James. Kinsey, William. Livingston, Stephen Crane, Richard. Smith, John De Hart*

Pennsylvania -- *Joseph Galloway, John Dickinson , Charles Humphreys, Thomas Mifflin, Edward Biddle, John Morton, George Ross*

The Lower Counties New Castl -- *Cæsar Rodney, Thomas. M: Kean, George Read*

Maryland -- *Matthew Tilghman, Thomas Johnson Junior, William Paca, Samuel Chase*

Virginia -- *Richard Henry Lee, George Washington, Patrick Henry, Junior, Richard Bland, Benjamin Harrison, Edmund Pendleton*

North-Carolina -- *William Hooper, Joseph Hewes, Richard Caswell*

South-Carolina -- *Henry Middleton, Thomas Lynch, Christopher Gadsden, John Rutledge, Edward Rutledge*

Chapter 10 Part II of II

The Articles of Association

History of the Articles of Association

God bless all the signers of the Articles of Association from all the thirteen states of the first union. A brave lot they were for sure. Where are brave Americans today in the mid period from 2010 to 2020? It seems most are sleeping as our country is in deep peril once again. The opposition is trying again to beat us by disarming us. Keep your guns, please!

The Articles of Association were written while the colonies hoped they could work out a deal with Britain so that freedom did not have to come from war. As a side note, the Brits knew the brave colonists were armed, and so even the mighty English walked gingerly in the colonies. .

As you can see by reading the Articles of Association, this document called on the colonies to stop importing goods from the British Isles beginning on December 1, 1774, if the Coercive Acts were not repealed. You may enjoy checking out the coercive acts (aka to some as the Intolerable Acts). Though this is not the thrust of this book, there is a very short historical synopsis in a chapter prior to the listing of the Articles in this chapter.

Should Britain fail to redress the colonists' grievances in a timely manner, this First Congress declared, then it would reconvene on May 10, 1775, and the colonies would cease to export goods to Britain on September 10, 1775. After proclaiming these measures, the First Continental Congress disbanded on October 26, 1774. Have you ever seen America so decisive? For me, the closest time other than this was the Cuban Missile Crisis!

Colonial Americans loved America and could not believe the British were going to hurt any American who wanted real freedom. They understood why the British were upset by the Boston Tea Party and other blatant acts of destruction of supposedly British property by American colonists. Yet, the colonists did not condone the British Acts, which forced America's hand.

Still thinking that the Americans would do whatever was demanded, the British Parliament enacted the Coercive Acts, as previously discussed, much to the outrage of American Patriots, on March 28, 1774.

Historians know that the Coercive Acts were a series of four acts established by the British government. The aim of the legislation was to restore order from the Crown's perspective in Massachusetts and to punish Bostonians big-time for their "Tea Party."

The British saw this "Tea Party" as an emboldened act by the revolutionary-minded Sons of Liberty, who had boarded three British tea ships in Boston Harbor and dumped 342 crates of tea—nearly $1 million worth in today's money—into the water to protest the Tea Act.

Since life had not improved and the British, after initially backing off from its taxation impositions, began to double down, continuing to impose its will on the colonists, Americans were ready for action. The Second Continental Congress began on May 10, 1775 and it went on until March 1, 1781.

During the Revolutionary war, the Second Congress continued, but its meeting location was moved from

Philadelphia several times to other locations to protect the lives of the representatives. Britain, as an adversary was not an easy foe with which to deal. The Americans needed to smarten up on the battlefield and so they looked for great generals, such as George Washington.

The English considered the American Revolution as tyranny, while the patriots in the colonies saw England's imposition of its strength upon the colonies as a tyrannical act that Americans could not tolerate.

The delegates from twelve of the thirteen original colonies gathered again in Philadelphia to discuss their next steps in dealing with England. This Second Congress met at the State House in Philadelphia (Now popularly known as Independence Hall) as the American Revolution had already begun in earnest with the shot heard round the world still ringing in their ears. After major deliberations in Georgia, this last colony finally joined the Congress, dispatching delegates who arrived on July 20, 1775.

When the Second Continental Congress came together on May 10, 1775 it was, in effect, a reconvening of the First Continental Congress. The Colonies sent many of the same 56 delegates who attended the first meeting. They appointed the same president (Peyton Randolph) and secretary (Charles Thomson). Some now famous new arrivals to Congress included Benjamin Franklin of Pennsylvania and John Hancock of Massachusetts.

Peyton Randolph, the President of Congress, a very important person in Virginia Politics, was summoned back to Virginia unexpectedly to preside over the House of Burgesses within two weeks of the convening of the 2nd Congress. Virginia sent Thomas Jefferson to replace him. He arrived several weeks later.

Henry Middleton was elected as President to replace Randolph, but he declined. John Hancock was then elected President of the Congress on May 24. One might say that John Hancock was the 2nd President of the United States (Peyton Randolph was the first) at a time when the country operated without a Constitution.

Massachusetts, which appears to have been the toughest state, had already organized the Minutemen. This was a special militia that could be ready on a minute's notice.

Minutemen skirmished with British troops at Lexington and Concord. Meanwhile, other farmer-soldiers joined them outside Boston to fight for America. The militia was still engaged in Boston while the Congress was using its powers to formally establish the Massachusetts militia as the Continental Army of the United States with George Washington of Virginia as the top general. The head of this army was known at the time as the Commander in Chief.

This marked another stage in the formation of the government of the US. The government would continue to evolve and after independence was gained, Washington would again become Commander in Chief when he was elected First President of the United States.

Sixty-five representatives originally appointed to the Second Continental Congress by the legislatures of thirteen British North American colonies accomplished a body of work that is historical in nature. At the time, it formed the basis for the new government, ready to take on and defeat England.

The Declaration of Independence, with text lightly referenced in Appendix C and detailed in the next chapter was the first well-known historical document produced by this Second Congress. The second was the Articles of Confederation, with text lightly referenced in Appendix D and shown in a subsequent chapter.

All of this great documentation of the strife of the colonists in their relationship with Britain is put forth in all of these documents, the intent of which at the time was to make America free. The Articles of Confederation was the precursor document to the United States Constitution, which is lightly referenced in Appendix E.

As noted previously, the Second Continental Congress was convened during the American Revolutionary War but prior to July 4, 1776. It served as the de facto U.S. national government as there was nothing else on the colonist side, as powerful. This Congress assumed power and raised armies, directed strategy, appointed diplomats, and it made the US government a formal entity.

At the same time, it produced numerous important documents, including three of the most fundamental and historical documents to American freedom—The Declaration of Independence, The Articles of Confederation, and The Constitution. We will cover these one by one in subsequent chapters.

Chapter 11

United States Declaration of Independence

By the Second Congress, July 4, 1776

Some dates, one can never forget. The Declaration of Independence was written by Thomas Jefferson, a relative newcomer and a real youngster, and it was put forth and approved for printing on July 4, 1776. It was a product of the Second Continental Congress. It did exactly what it purported to do in its title. It declared independence from Great Britain.

It was not Pennsylvania, or Massachusetts or Virginia that declared this independence and this is a key point. Instead, it was all of the thirteen colonies in unison, known to themselves as states at the time. They had chosen to assemble and join in a union to create a new federal government that would one day be known as the United States of America.

Once independence was declared, America began to legally operate fully independent of the Crown with its own government. Considering that the colonists were in revolt and war had commenced, it is an understatement to suggest that the colonists were not operating independently prior to the Declaration. The Declaration formalized their union of independence.

The states were declared to be free and independent and "all political connection between them and the State of Great

Britain, is and ought to be totally dissolved." The formal title of the document ratified on July 4, 1776 is the "Unanimous Declaration of the thirteen United States of America," but to Americans it is known simply as the Declaration of Independence. This was the formal end of the thirteen colonies.

Larger original paragraphs are sometimes decomposed into several to make the material in the Declaration more readable. No words were changed other than spelling. The contents of the full Declaration of Independence and any explanations are provided immediately below and an explanation of the text is provided at the end of this chapter.

The Declaration of Independence

IN CONGRESS, JULY 4, 1776

The Unanimous Declaration of the thirteen united States of America

When in the Course of human events it becomes necessary for one people to dissolve the political bands which have connected them with another and to assume among the powers of the earth, the separate and equal station to which the Laws of Nature and of Nature's God entitle them, a decent respect to the opinions of mankind requires that they should declare the causes which impel them to the separation.

We hold these truths to be self-evident, that all men are created equal, that they are endowed by their Creator with certain unalienable Rights, that among these are Life, Liberty and the pursuit of Happiness. — That to secure these rights, Governments are instituted among Men, deriving their just powers from the consent of the governed, — That whenever any Form of Government becomes destructive of these ends, it is the Right of the People to alter or to abolish it, and to institute new Government, laying its foundation on such principles and organizing its powers in such form, as to them shall seem most likely to affect their Safety and Happiness.

Prudence, indeed, will dictate that Governments long established should not be changed for light and transient causes; and accordingly all experience hath shewn that mankind are more disposed to suffer, while evils are sufferable than to right themselves by abolishing the forms to which they are accustomed.

But when a long train of abuses and usurpations, pursuing invariably the same Object evinces a design to reduce them under absolute Despotism, it is their right, it is their duty, to throw off such Government, and to provide new Guards for their future security. — Such has been the patient sufferance of these Colonies; and such is now the necessity which constrains them to alter their former Systems of Government.

The history of the present King of Great Britain is a history of repeated injuries and usurpations, all having in direct object the establishment of an absolute Tyranny over these States. To prove this, let Facts be submitted to a candid world.

He has refused his Assent to Laws, the most wholesome and necessary for the public good.

He has forbidden his Governors to pass Laws of immediate and pressing importance, unless suspended in their operation till his Assent should be obtained; and when so suspended, he has utterly neglected to attend to them.

He has refused to pass other Laws for the accommodation of large districts of people, unless those people would relinquish the right of Representation in the Legislature, a right inestimable to them and formidable to tyrants only.

He has called together legislative bodies at places unusual, uncomfortable, and distant from the depository of their Public Records, for the sole purpose of fatiguing them into compliance with his measures.

He has dissolved Representative Houses repeatedly, for opposing with manly firmness his invasions on the rights of the people.

He has refused for a long time, after such dissolutions, to cause others to be elected, whereby the Legislative Powers, incapable of Annihilation, have returned to the People at large for their exercise; the State remaining in the mean time exposed to all the dangers of invasion from without, and convulsions within.

He has endeavored to prevent the population of these States; for that purpose obstructing the Laws for Naturalization of Foreigners; refusing to pass others to encourage their migrations hither, and raising the conditions of new Appropriations of Lands.

He has obstructed the Administration of Justice by refusing his Assent to Laws for establishing Judiciary Powers.

He has made Judges dependent on his Will alone for the tenure of their offices, and the amount and payment of their salaries.

He has erected a multitude of New Offices, and sent hither swarms of Officers to harass our people and eat out their substance.

He has kept among us, in times of peace, Standing Armies without the Consent of our legislatures.

He has affected to render the Military independent of and superior to the Civil Power.

He has combined with others to subject us to a jurisdiction foreign to our constitution, and unacknowledged by our laws; giving his Assent to their Acts of pretended Legislation:

> *For quartering large bodies of armed troops among us:*

> *For protecting them, by a mock Trial from punishment for any Murders which they should commit on the Inhabitants of these States:*

> *For cutting off our Trade with all parts of the world:*

> *For imposing Taxes on us without our Consent:*

> *For depriving us in many cases, of the benefit of Trial by Jury:*

> *For transporting us beyond Seas to be tried for pretended offences:*

> *For abolishing the free System of English Laws in a neighboring Province, establishing therein an Arbitrary government, and enlarging its Boundaries so as to render it at once an example and fit instrument for introducing the same absolute rule into these Colonies*

> *For taking away our Charters, abolishing our most valuable Laws and altering fundamentally the Forms of our Governments:*

For suspending our own Legislatures, and declaring themselves invested with power to legislate for us in all cases whatsoever.

He has abdicated Government here, by declaring us out of his Protection and waging War against us.

He has plundered our seas, ravaged our coasts, burnt our towns, and destroyed the lives of our people.

He is at this time transporting large Armies of foreign Mercenaries to complete the works of death, desolation, and tyranny, already begun with circumstances of Cruelty & Perfidy scarcely paralleled in the most barbarous ages, and totally unworthy the Head of a civilized nation.

He has constrained our fellow Citizens taken Captive on the high Seas to bear Arms against their Country, to become the executioners of their friends and Brethren, or to fall themselves by their Hands.

He has excited domestic insurrections amongst us, and has endeavored to bring on the inhabitants of our frontiers, the merciless Indian Savages whose known rule of warfare, is an undistinguished destruction of all ages, sexes and conditions.

[As you can see, the Patriots were quite annoyed with the King!]

In every stage of these Oppressions We have Petitioned for Redress in the most humble terms: Our repeated Petitions have been answered only by repeated injury. A Prince, whose character is thus marked by every act which may define a Tyrant, is unfit to be the ruler of a free people.

Nor have We been wanting in attentions to our British brethren. We have warned them from time to time of attempts by their legislature to extend an unwarrantable jurisdiction over us. We have reminded them of the circumstances of our emigration and settlement here. We have appealed to their native justice and magnanimity, and we have conjured them by the ties of our common kindred to disavow these usurpations, which would inevitably interrupt our connections and correspondence.

They too have been deaf to the voice of justice and of consanguinity. We must, therefore, acquiesce in the necessity, which denounces our Separation, and hold them, as we hold the rest of mankind, Enemies in War, in Peace Friends.

We, therefore, the Representatives of the united States of America, in General Congress, Assembled, appealing to the Supreme Judge of the world for the rectitude of our intentions, do, in the Name, and by Authority of the good People of these Colonies, solemnly publish and declare, That these united Colonies are, and of Right ought to be Free and Independent States, that they are Absolved from all Allegiance to the British Crown, and that all political connection between them and the State of Great Britain, is and ought to be totally dissolved; and that as Free and Independent States, they have full Power to levy War, conclude Peace, contract Alliances, establish Commerce, and to do all other Acts and Things which Independent States may of right do. — And for the support of this Declaration, with a firm reliance on the protection of Divine Providence, we mutually pledge to each other our Lives, our Fortunes, and our sacred Honor.

— John Hancock

New Hampshire: Josiah Bartlett, William Whipple, Matthew Thornton

Massachusetts: John Hancock, Samuel Adams, John Adams, Robert Treat Paine, Elbridge Gerry

Rhode Island: Stephen Hopkins, William Ellery

Connecticut: Roger Sherman, Samuel Huntington, William Williams, Oliver Wolcott

New York: William Floyd, Philip Livingston, Francis Lewis, Lewis Morris

New Jersey: Richard Stockton, John Witherspoon, Francis Hopkinson, John Hart, Abraham Clark

Pennsylvania: Robert Morris, Benjamin Rush, Benjamin Franklin, John Morton, George Clymer, James Smith, George Taylor, James Wilson, George Ross

Delaware: Caesar Rodney, George Read, Thomas McKean

Maryland: Samuel Chase, William Paca, Thomas Stone, Charles Carroll of Carrollton

Virginia: George Wythe, Richard Henry Lee, Thomas Jefferson, Benjamin Harrison, Thomas Nelson, Jr., Francis Lightfoot Lee, Carter Braxton

North Carolina: William Hooper, Joseph Hewes, John Penn

South Carolina: Edward Rutledge, Thomas Heyward, Jr., Thomas Lynch, Jr., Arthur Middleton

Georgia: Button Gwinnett, Lyman Hall, George Walton

End-of-Declaration

Declaration of Independence – Explanation and Additional Thoughts

In addition to declaring independence, this document gave justification for the separation from the Crown in sufficient detail that the King and Parliament could not misunderstand its purpose and from whence it came. Since the colonies were no more, historians consider this Declaration as the founding document of the United States of America. In his Gettysburg Address of 1863, at the beginning of his address, President Lincoln memorialized the founding of the United States in these words:

Four score and seven years ago our fathers brought forth on this continent, a new nation, conceived in liberty, and dedicated to the proposition that all men are created equal.

And so, though some contest it, as the founding document, the Declaration of Independence still is in effect. Along with the essence of the Constitution and ninth amendment it gives the rights to the people, including rights not discovered at the time of the writing.

As we know from our knowledge of American History and its recount of the Revolutionary War, there were a number of battles until the Americans prevailed in the war with England. After the Declaration of Independence, the Second Continental Congress stayed in session, meeting periodically, passing laws and drafting other documents that ultimately would define the new nation as the United States of America.

The next major document in the formation of the government of the United States is known as *The Articles of Confederation.* These Articles served as the defining document of rules until a "more perfect union was formed with the writing and the adoption of the US Constitution. Until The Constitution, the Articles of Confederation were the Law of the Land.

Chapter 12

United States Articles of Confederation Part I of III

Introduction & Articles I through VII

Written and adopted by the Second Congress, November 15, 1777

The Second Continental Congress adopted the Articles of Confederation, the first "constitution" of the United States, on November 15, 1777. However, ratification of the Articles of Confederation by all thirteen states did not occur until March 1, 1781.

Just as the Declaration of Independence is short for a longer title, the "Articles of Confederation and Perpetual Union" has been shortened over time to be simply The Articles of Confederation. Some say that the Articles of Confederation represent the United States of America's first constitution. After the Second Continental Congress, the Articles established a "firm league of friendship," which is affirmed as a not too trivial perpetual union between and among the 13 about-to-be-united states.

After having been subjected to the wiles of the strong central government of the British prior to the War of Independence, these Articles reflect a sense of the wariness by the states of a government that would not provide them with their God-given rights.

The Articles are the agreed-upon remedy for the concerns of states' rights and for individual rights. Ever fearful that a government of the future (such as the current regime or one hence) might not have the right measure of concern for our individual needs if it were given too much power, and that abuses such as the Intolerable Acts, might again be the result, the Articles purposely established a guiding set of rules / laws, which in essence was a "constitution."

In presenting the Articles, larger paragraphs are sometimes decomposed into several to make the material more readable. The full contents of the Articles of Confederation and any explanations are provided immediately below. First we show the cover text; then a facsimile of the original cover.

ARTICLES
OF
CONFEDERATION
AND
PERPETUAL UNION
BETWEEN
THE
STATES
OF
NEW HAMPSHIRE, MASSACHUSETTS-BAY RHODE ISLAND AND
PROVIDENCE PLANTATIONS, CONNECTICUT, NEW YORK, NEW
JERSEY, PENNSYLVANIA, DELAWARE, MARYLAND, VIRGINIA,
NORTH CAROLINA, SOUTH CAROLINA AND GEORGIA

WILLIAMSBURG:
Printed by Alexander Purdie

Now, here is how a copy of how the cover looked many years after it was printed:

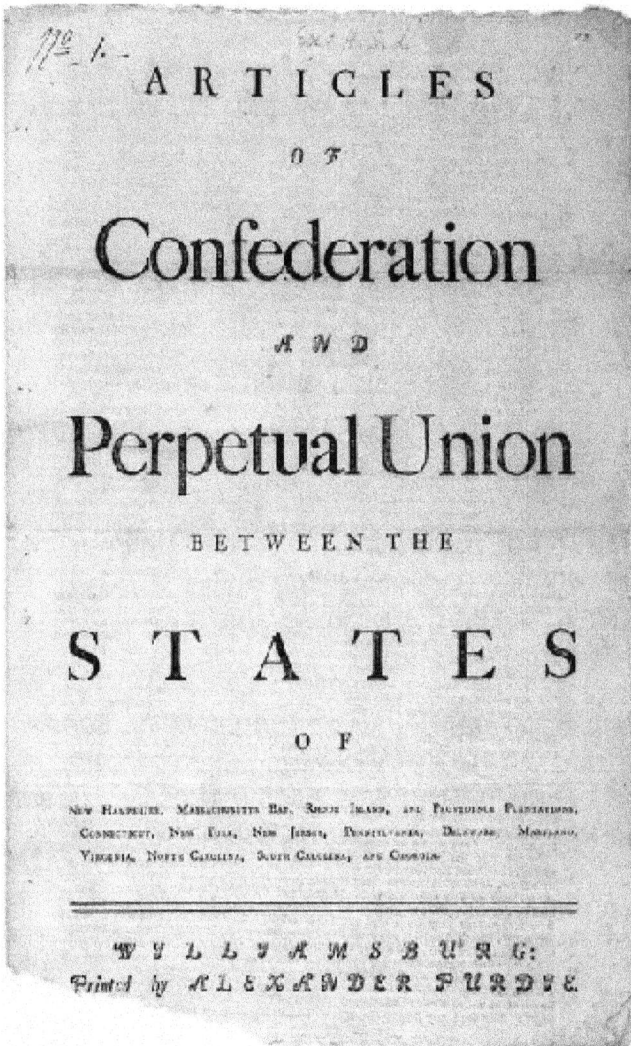

The Text and Explanations of The Articles of Confederation follow:

Agreed to by Congress November 15, 1777; ratified and in force, March 1, 1781.

Preamble:

To all to whom these Presents shall come, we the undersigned Delegates of the States affixed to our Names send greeting.

Articles of Confederation and perpetual Union between the States of New Hampshire, Massachusetts bay, Rhode Island and Providence Plantations, Connecticut, New York, New Jersey, Pennsylvania, Delaware, Maryland, Virginia, North Carolina, South Carolina and Georgia.

Article I. *The Style of this Confederacy shall be "The United States of America."*

[Explanation of Article I: This Article confirms the name of the new nation as "The United States of America." This "new" name first appeared in the Declaration of Independence.**]**

Article II. *Each state retains its sovereignty, freedom, and independence, and every power, jurisdiction, and right, which is not by this Confederation expressly delegated to the United States, in Congress assembled.*

[Explanation of Article II: This Article affirms that each state is a sovereign and independent state and retains all powers not granted to the Congress. In other words if any power is omnipotent, it resides in the individual states.]

Article III. *The said States hereby severally enter into a firm league of friendship with each other, for their common defense, the security of their liberties, and their mutual and general welfare, binding themselves to assist each other, against all force offered to, or attacks made upon them, or any of them, on account of religion, sovereignty, trade, or any other pretense whatever.*

[**Explanation of Article IV:** This Article affirms a "league of friendship," and it binds all states into a common defense pact. From this point on the "states" are united.]

Article IV. *The better to secure and perpetuate mutual friendship and intercourse among the people of the different States in this Union, the free inhabitants of each of these States, paupers, vagabonds, and fugitives from justice excepted, shall be entitled to all privileges and immunities of free citizens in the several States; and the people of each State shall [have] free ingress and regress to and from any other State, and shall enjoy therein all the privileges of trade and commerce, subject to the same duties, impositions, and restrictions as the inhabitants thereof respectively, provided that such restrictions shall not extend so far as to prevent the removal of property imported into any State, to any other State, of which the owner is an inhabitant; provided also that no imposition, duties or restriction shall be laid by any State, on the property of the United States, or either of them.*

If any person guilty of, or charged with, treason, felony, or other high misdemeanor in any State, shall flee from justice, and be found in any of the United States, he shall, upon demand of the Governor or executive power of the State from which he fled, be delivered up and removed to the State having jurisdiction of his offense.

Full faith and credit shall be given in each of these States to the records, acts, and judicial proceedings of the courts and magistrates of every other State.

[**Explanation of Article IV**: This is an important article in that it is continued to the Constitution in its Article IV. It is obscure and complicated enough to require an explanation. It ensures that when a citizen of one state travels in or through another state, the person shall enjoy all the rights of the citizens of the state he or she is traveling through. It also ensures free travel between the states. It requires a state to hand over a fugitive from justice who has fled to that state. Finally, it requires that full faith and credit by given to the records and acts of one state by all other states.]

[As previously noted, most of the provisions of Article IV were carried over into the Constitution in its Article IV.]

Article V. *For the most convenient management of the general interests of the United States, delegates shall be annually appointed in such manner as the legislatures of each State shall direct, to meet in Congress on the first Monday in November, in every year, with a power reserved to each State to recall its delegates, or any of them, at any time within the year, and to send others in their stead for the remainder of the year.*

No State shall be represented in Congress by less than two, nor more than seven members; and no person shall be capable of being a delegate for more than three years in any term of six years; nor shall any person, being a delegate, be capable of holding any office under the United States, for which he, or another for his benefit, receives any salary, fees or emolument of any kind.

Each State shall maintain its own delegates in a meeting of the States, and while they act as members of the committee of the States.

In determining questions in the United States in Congress assembled, each State shall have one vote.

Freedom of speech and debate in Congress shall not be impeached or questioned in any court or place out of Congress, and the members of Congress shall be protected in their persons from arrests or imprisonments, during the time of their going to and from, and attendance on Congress, except for treason, felony, or breach of the peace.

[Explanation of Article V: This Article establishes that the Congress is to consist of one chamber, as a unicameral legislature known as the "The United States in Congress Assembled". Unlike the Congress defined by the Constitution which is a bicameral, two house (Senate and House of Representatives) in this, there would be just one intact Congress.

Each state legislature would choose its own congressional delegates and they were free to send from two to seven members. The people's vote came from their sate's legislators, elected by the people. Delegates had a term limit of no more than three years every six years. [Great idea – term limits] When a vote came to the floor of the Congress, each of the state delegates would meet to determine the state's one vote - states voted as states, individual members of Congress did not vote as individuals.

Article V also provides the freedom of speech to all members of Congress while in Congress. It also gives immunity to all members of Congress for whatever is spoken in Congress. Additionally, this Article saves from harm all members of Congress to be free from arrest while traveling to and from Congress.]

Article VI. *No State, without the consent of the United States in Congress assembled, shall send any embassy to, or receive any embassy from, or enter into any conference, agreement, alliance or treaty with any King, Prince or State; nor shall any person holding any office of profit or trust under the United States, or any of them, accept any present, emolument, office or title of any kind whatever from any King, Prince or foreign State; nor shall the United States in Congress assembled, or any of them, grant any title of nobility.*

No two or more States shall enter into any treaty, confederation or alliance whatever between them, without the consent of the United States in Congress assembled, specifying accurately the purposes for which the same is to be entered into, and how long it shall continue.

No State shall lay any imposts or duties, which may interfere with any stipulations in treaties, entered into by the United States in Congress assembled, with any King, Prince or State, in pursuance of any treaties already proposed by Congress, to the courts of France and Spain.

No vessel of war shall be kept up in time of peace by any State, except such number only, as shall be deemed necessary by the United States in Congress assembled, for the defense of such State, or its trade; nor shall any body of forces be kept up by any State in time of peace, except such number only, as in the judgment of the United States in Congress assembled, shall be deemed requisite to garrison the forts necessary for the defense of such State; but every State shall always keep up a well-regulated and disciplined militia, sufficiently armed and accoutered, and shall provide and constantly have ready for use, in public stores, a due number of filed pieces and tents, and a proper quantity of arms, ammunition and camp equipage.

No State shall engage in any war without the consent of the United States in Congress assembled, unless such State be actually invaded by enemies, or shall have received certain advice of a resolution being formed by some nation of Indians to invade such State, and the danger is so imminent as not to admit of a delay till the United States in Congress assembled can be consulted; nor shall any State grant commissions to any ships or vessels of war, nor letters of marque or reprisal,

…except it be after a declaration of war by the United States in Congress assembled, and then only against the Kingdom or State and the subjects thereof, against which war has been so declared, and under such regulations as shall be established by the United States in Congress assembled, unless such State be infested by pirates, in

which case vessels of war may be fitted out for that occasion, and kept so long as the danger shall continue, or until the United States in Congress assembled shall determine otherwise.

[Explanation of Article VI: This Article places limits on the states. Other than all limits specifically noted, state power was unlimited and federal (Central Government of the US) was totally limited. Specifically they are as follows:

No state could enter into a treaty without the consent of Congress

No state could grant a title of nobility (nor would Congress)

No vessels of war could be kept in peacetime, except that number determined by Congress necessary for defense

No state could engage in a war except on the authorization of Congress, unless invaded or in danger of invasion]

Article VII. *When land forces are raised by any State for the common defense, all officers of or under the rank of colonel, shall be appointed by the legislature of each State respectively, by whom such forces shall be raised, or in such manner as such State shall direct, and all vacancies shall be filled up by the State which first made the appointment.*

[Explanation of Article VII : This article ensures that all military officers of the state militias, at the rank of colonel or below, were to be appointed by the state legislature.]

Chapter 12

United States Articles of Confederation Part II of III

Articles VIII through X

Article VIII. *All charges of war, and all other expenses that shall be incurred for the common defense or general welfare, and allowed by the United States in Congress assembled, shall be defrayed out of a common treasury, which shall be supplied by the several States in proportion to the value of all land within each State, granted or surveyed for any person, as such land and the buildings and improvements thereon shall be estimated according to such mode as the United States in Congress assembled, shall from time to time direct and appoint.*

The taxes for paying that proportion shall be laid and levied by the authority and direction of the legislatures of the several States within the time agreed upon by the United States in Congress assembled.

[**Explanation of Article VIII:** This Article directs that any expenses of the United States are to be paid out of a common treasury, with deposits made to the treasury by the states in proportion to the value of the land and buildings in the state.

No country can exist without a guaranteed source of funding. The Articles unfortunately provided no way to fund the country as there was no way for the National Congress to force the states to pay this levy. It was one of the major weaknesses of the Articles of Confederation corrected by the Constitution which came years later.]

Article IX. *The United States in Congress assembled, shall have the sole and exclusive right and power of determining on peace and war, except in the cases mentioned in the sixth article*
  — *of sending and receiving ambassadors*
  — *entering into treaties and alliances, provided that no treaty of commerce shall be made whereby the legislative power of the respective States shall be restrained from imposing such imposts and duties on foreigners, as their own people are subjected to, or from prohibiting the exportation or importation of any species of goods or commodities whatsoever*
  — *of establishing rules for deciding in all cases, what captures on land or water shall be legal, and in what manner prizes taken by land or naval forces in the service of the United States shall be divided or appropriated*
  — *of granting letters of marque and reprisal in times of peace*
  — *appointing courts for the trial of piracies and felonies committed on the high seas and establishing courts for receiving and determining finally appeals in all cases of captures, provided that no member of Congress shall be appointed a judge of any of the said courts.*

The United States in Congress assembled shall also be the last resort on appeal in all disputes and differences now subsisting or that hereafter may arise between two or more States concerning boundary, jurisdiction or any other causes whatever; which authority shall always be exercised in the manner following.

Whenever the legislative or executive authority or lawful agent of any State in controversy with another shall present a petition to Congress stating the matter in question and praying for a hearing, notice thereof shall be given by order of Congress to the legislative or executive authority of the other State in controversy, and a day assigned for the appearance of the parties by their lawful agents, who shall then be directed to appoint by joint consent, commissioners or judges to constitute a court for hearing and determining the matter in question:

but if they cannot agree,

Congress shall name three persons out of each of the United States, and from the list of such persons each party shall alternately strike out one, the petitioners beginning, until the number shall be reduced to thirteen; and from that number not less than seven, nor more than nine names as Congress shall direct, shall in the presence of Congress be drawn out by lot, and the persons whose names shall be so drawn or any five of them, shall be commissioners or judges, to hear and finally determine the controversy,

so always as a major part of the judges who shall hear the cause shall agree in the determination: and if either party shall neglect to attend at the day appointed, without showing reasons, which Congress shall judge sufficient, or being present shall refuse to strike, the Congress shall proceed to nominate three persons out of each State, and the secretary of Congress shall strike in behalf of such party absent or refusing;

and the judgment and sentence of the court to be appointed, in the manner before prescribed, shall be final and conclusive; and if any of the parties shall refuse to submit to the authority of such court, or to appear or defend their claim or cause, the court shall nevertheless proceed to pronounce sentence, or judgment, which shall in like manner be final and decisive, the judgment or sentence and other proceedings being in either case transmitted to

Congress, and lodged among the acts of Congress for the security of the parties concerned:

provided that every commissioner, before he sits in judgment, shall take an oath to be administered by one of the judges of the supreme or superior court of the State, where the cause shall be tried, 'well and truly to hear and determine the matter in question, according to the best of his judgment, without favor, affection or hope of reward': provided also, that no State shall be deprived of territory for the benefit of the United States.

All controversies concerning the private right of soil claimed under different grants of two or more States, whose jurisdictions as they may respect such lands, and the States which passed such grants are adjusted, the said grants or either of them being at the same time claimed to have originated antecedent to such settlement of jurisdiction, shall on the petition of either party to the Congress of the United States, be finally determined as near as may be in the same manner as is before prescribed for deciding disputes respecting territorial jurisdiction between different States.

The United States in Congress assembled shall also have the sole and exclusive right and power of regulating the alloy and value of coin struck by their own authority, or by that of the respective States

- *fixing the standards of weights and measures throughout the United States*
- *regulating the trade and managing all affairs with the Indians, not members of any of the States, provided that the legislative right of any State within its own limits be not infringed or violated*
- *establishing or regulating post offices from one State to another, throughout all the United States, and exacting such postage on the papers passing through the same as may be requisite to defray the expenses of the said office*

— *appointing all officers of the land forces, in the service of the United States, excepting regimental officers*
— *appointing all the officers of the naval forces, and commissioning all officers whatever in the service of the United States*
— *making rules for the government and regulation of the said land and naval forces, and directing their operations.*

The United States in Congress assembled shall have authority to appoint a committee, to sit in the recess of Congress, to be denominated 'A Committee of the States', and to consist of one delegate from each State; and to appoint such other committees and civil officers as may be necessary for managing the general affairs of the United States under their direction

— *to appoint one of their members to preside, provided that no person be allowed to serve in the office of president more than one year in any term of three years; to ascertain the necessary sums of money to be raised for the service of the United States, and to appropriate and apply the same for defraying the public expenses*
— *to borrow money, or emit bills on the credit of the United States, transmitting every half-year to the respective States an account of the sums of money so borrowed or emitted — to build and equip a navy*
— *to agree upon the number of land forces, and to make requisitions from each State for its quota, in proportion to the number of white inhabitants in such State; which requisition shall be binding, and thereupon the legislature of each State shall appoint the regimental officers, raise the men and cloath, arm and equip them in a solid- like manner, at the expense of the United States; and the officers and men so clothed, armed and equipped shall march to*

the place appointed, and within the time agreed on by the United States in Congress assembled. But if the United States in Congress assembled shall, on consideration of circumstances judge proper that any State should not raise men, or should raise a smaller number of men than the quota thereof, such extra number shall be raised, officered, clothed, armed and equipped in the same manner as the quota of each State, unless the legislature of such State shall judge that such extra number cannot be safely spread out in the same, in which case they shall raise, officer, clothe, arm and equip as many of such extra number as they judge can be safely spared. And the officers and men so clothed, armed, and equipped, shall march to the place appointed, and within the time agreed on by the United States in Congress assembled.

The United States in Congress assembled shall never engage in a war, nor grant letters of marque or reprisal in time of peace, nor enter into any treaties or alliances, nor coin money, nor regulate the value thereof, nor ascertain the sums and expenses necessary for the defense and welfare of the United States, or any of them, nor emit bills, nor borrow money on the credit of the United States, nor appropriate money, nor agree upon the number of vessels of war, to be built or purchased, or the number of land or sea forces to be raised, nor appoint a commander in chief of the army or navy,

unless nine States assent to the same: nor shall a question on any other point, except for adjourning from day to day be determined, unless by the votes of the majority of the United States in Congress assembled.

The Congress of the United States shall have power to adjourn to any time within the year, and to any place within the United States, so that no period of adjournment be for a longer duration than the space of six months, and shall publish the journal of their proceedings monthly, except such parts thereof relating to treaties, alliances or military operations, as in their judgment require secrecy;

and the yeas and nays of the delegates of each State on any question shall be entered on the journal, when it is desired by any delegates of a State, or any of them, at his or their request shall be furnished with a transcript of the said journal, except such parts as are above excepted, to lay before the legislatures of the several States.

[Explanation of Article IX: This Article is very large and very explicit. It lists the specific powers of the Congress of the Central Government of the United States. The states by definition had all other powers. The powers as determined were as follows:

the power to declare war and peace
the power to send and receive ambassadors
the power to make treaties
the power to grant letters of marque
the power to regulate the currency of the United States and the individual states
the power to fix standards and measures
the power to establish post offices
the power to make rules for land and naval forces
the power to borrow money on the behalf of the United States
the power to build and equip a navy
the power to determine the size of an army and to requisition troops from each state to fill the need
the power to arm, equip, and clothe the members of the army

This Article also makes Congress the final court of appeal for disputes between states. All decisions of the Congress must be been made by majority vote of the states.

Additionally, it establishes "A Committee of the States," which takes the place of the full Congress when it is not in session. This committee was made up of one member of

Congress from each state. The notion of an Executive Branch as in the Constitution had not yet been codified.

This Article also directs Congress to choose one of its number to be presiding officer (to be chosen for one year, and with a service limit of one year out of three). This person, often referred to as "President," had a role much akin to the Speaker of the House of the House of Representatives under the Constitution. Though at the time, there was no "President of the United States" as we now understand them.

The Congress was required to meet at least once a year, and could adjourn at any time, though never for more than six months at a time. This article also requires Congress to publish its proceedings and the results of all votes taken for history.]

Chapter 12

United States Articles of Confederation Part III of III

Articles X through XIII

Article X. *The Committee of the States, or any nine of them, shall be authorized to execute, in the recess of Congress, such of the powers of Congress as the United States in Congress assembled, by the consent of the nine States, shall from time to time think expedient to vest them with; provided that no power be delegated to the said Committee, for the exercise of which, by the Articles of Confederation, the voice of nine States in the Congress of the United States assembled be requisite.*

[**Explanation of Article X:** This Article allows the Committee of the States, or any nine individual states, to make decisions for the United States when Congress is in adjournment.]

Article XI. *Canada acceding to this confederation, and adjoining in the measures of the United States, shall be admitted into, and entitled to all the advantages of this Union; but no other colony shall be admitted into the same, unless such admission be agreed to by nine States.*

[**Explanation of Article XI:** This Article invites Canada to join the United States as a new state, at any time. Other new states, however, must be approved by the vote of nine existing states.]

Article XII. *All bills of credit emitted, monies borrowed, and debts contracted by, or under the authority of Congress, before the assembling of the United States, in pursuance of the present confederation, shall be deemed and considered as a charge against the United States, for payment and satisfaction whereof the said United States, and the public faith are hereby solemnly pledged.*

[**Explanation of Article XII:** This Article ensures that all debt incurred by the Continental Congresses assembled before the Articles went into effect would be valid and binding on the United States.]

Article XIII. *Every State shall abide by the determination of the United States in Congress assembled, on all questions which by this confederation are submitted to them. And the Articles of this Confederation shall be inviolably observed by every State, and the Union shall be perpetual; nor shall any alteration at any time hereafter be made in any of them; unless such alteration be agreed to in a Congress of the United States, and be afterwards confirmed by the legislatures of every State.*

[**Explanation of Article XIII:** This Article requires the states to be held to the decisions of Congress; it notes that the union is perpetual; and that any changes to the Articles must be agreed upon by Congress and all states.]

Continuation of the Articles of Confederation

And Whereas it hath pleased the Great Governor of the World to incline the hearts of the legislatures we respectively represent in Congress, to approve of, and to authorize us to ratify the said Articles of Confederation and perpetual Union. Know Ye that we the undersigned delegates, by virtue of the power and authority to us given for that purpose, do by these presents, in the name and in behalf of our respective constituents, fully and entirely ratify and confirm each and every of the said Articles of Confederation and perpetual Union, and all and singular the matters and things therein contained:

And we do further solemnly plight and engage the faith of our respective constituents, that they shall abide by the determinations of the United States in Congress assembled, on all questions, which by the said Confederation are submitted to them. And that the Articles thereof shall be inviolably observed by the States we respectively represent, and that the Union shall be perpetual.

In Witness whereof we have hereunto set our hands in Congress. Done at Philadelphia in the State of Pennsylvania the ninth day of July in the Year of our Lord One Thousand Seven Hundred and Seventy-Eight, and in the Third Year of the independence of America.

On the part and behalf of the State of New Hampshire:
Josiah Bartlett, John Wentworth Junior. August 8th 1778

On the part and behalf of The State of Massachusetts Bay:
John Hancock, Samuel Adams, Elbridge Gerry, Francis Dana, James Lovell, Samuel Holten

On the part and behalf of the State of Rhode Island and Providence Plantations:
William Ellery, Henry Marchant, John Collins

On the part and behalf of the State of Connecticut:
Roger Sherman, Samuel Huntington, Oliver Wolcott, Titus Hosmer, Andrew Adams

On the part and behalf of the State of New York:
James Duane, Francis Lewis, William Duer, Gouv Morris

On the part and behalf of the State of New Jersey: John Witherspoon, Nathan Scudder --November 26, 1778.

On the part and behalf of the State of Pennsylvania:
Robert Morris, Daniel Roberdeau, John Bayard Smith, William Clingan, Joseph Reed -- 22nd July 1778

On the part and behalf of the State of Delaware:
Thomas Mckean February 12, 1779, John Dickinson May 5th 1779, Nicholas Van Dyke

On the part and behalf of the State of Maryland:
John Hanson March 1 1781, Daniel Carroll

On the part and behalf of the State of Virginia:
Richard Henry Lee, John Banister, Thomas Adams, John Harvie,
Francis Lightfoot Lee

On the part and behalf of the State of North Carolina:
John Penn July 21st 1778, Cornelius Harnett, John Williams

On the part and behalf of the State of South Carolina:
Henry Laurens, William Henry Drayton, John Mathews, Richard Hutson,
Thomas Heyward Junior

On the part and behalf of the State of Georgia:
John Walton 24th July 1778, Edward Telfair, Edward Langworthy

--end of the Articles of Confederation text and explanation--

Articles of Confederation—Another Look!

When analyzed correctly, the Articles of Confederation vested
the largest share of power to the individual states. When the
Constitution was built and later enacted, it reflected the same
notion of states' rights and individual rights, as the Articles,
and the last claimant on the rights list was the federal
government in Washington. The founders abhorred the notion
of a strong central government such as a monarchy—like that
of England's George III.

Under the Articles of Confederation, each of the states
retained its "sovereignty, freedom and independence." The
preamble of the US Constitution drafted in 1787 and ratified
later by the individual states one at a time, sets its purpose as
"in order to form a more perfect union."

The founders of our government recognized that there were
flaws in the Articles of Confederation that would more easily
permit a tyranny to take place. And, so their best, "more
perfect" work, the Constitution, was their way of correcting
those flaws and correcting the notion of a constitutional
representative democracy (aka, a Republic) for the United
States.

There was a permanent institution called the Congress formed in the Articles as a national legislature comprised of representatives of the states. The Congress was responsible for conducting foreign affairs, declaring war or peace, maintaining an army and navy and a variety of other lesser functions.

The Articles did not call for the separation of powers with an executive, legislative, and judicial branch. The Articles did not permit the delegates **to collect taxes, regulate interstate commerce and enforce laws.** Under the Articles of Confederation these important functions could only be performed by the central government if the states agreed, and for as long as the states agreed.

Though the Articles had shortcomings, this historical and functional document provided the guidelines for the United States government and it was the only real law of the land until the Constitution was adopted and ratified.

Eventually, the shortcomings were addressed and this lead to the U.S. Constitution. The beauty of the Articles of Confederation was that they provided a workable framework during those years in which the 13 states were struggling to achieve their independent status.

Considering that the Constitution itself is under fire today by those who would like it constructed in ways that were not intended by the Founding Fathers, from November 15, 1777, when adopted by the Congress, the Articles of Confederation did their job to keep the Country in good stead. Nothing in life worth having is easy.

On March1, 1781, the Articles became operational when the last of the thirteen states signed the document. The next happening was the work of the Framers to create the US Constitution.

Part IV The Most Patriotic Document: The Constitution

Chapter 13

The Constitution, An Awesome Document Part I of VI

Introduction to the Constitution

The Articles of Confederation were admittedly an imperfect *constitution* for the newly formed union. To put this in proper perspective, would it have been possible for Bill Gates to have introduced Windows 8 in 1985 rather than Windows 1.0? That answer is a clear no.

Mr. Gates and Microsoft needed to go through all of the versions from 1.0 to Windows 8 to learn what was needed in Windows 8. This is similar to how The Constitution is a better version of the first law of the land, the Articles of Confederation. Once there is a basis for something, it can be improved. The Articles were well done but needed improvement.

The additional features in the Constitution over the Articles of Confederation are substantial. In many ways it was like going from Windows 1.0 to Windows 98. Then, of course the Bill of rights was like moving to Windows NT from 98. Now, add in the 17 other constitutional amendments, each a minor update to the Constitution, and we can ask ourselves in Microsoft parlance, "What version of the Constitution are we running today?

As an aside, besides the powers of government being separated, which items gave the government a higher probability for tyranny? George Washington described the biggest problem with the Articles of Confederation in just two words, "no money."

The Federal government relied on the states for funding. Without the Constitution, America might really be the name of a large land mass with 48 countries, and two not contiguous countries--Hawaii and Alaska. A country with no money could not survive over the long haul.

The barebones Constitution itself was far more perfect than the Articles of Confederation, just like Windows 98 was far more perfect than Windows 1.0. Microsoft could not immediately go to Windows 8 because nobody knew how any of the other previous versions would behave or be accepted, and all the subsequent iterations of Windows occurred from its use over time, and its technological successes and failings.

In many ways, our country grew the same way. The phrase "a more perfect union" in the Preamble of the Constitution notes the imperfections in a prior version and it introduces the rationale for the drawing of the Constitution. We know from reading the prior chapter that the prior document was The Articles of Confederation. Bill Gates knew that the prior document to Windows was the last version of DOS without the Windows GUI. He knew he could make it better.

The U.S. Constitution (and its subsequent 27 amendments) mimics the idea of having a v3.1, V4.1.x, and V5.x.3. It has survived for over well over two-hundred years without many changes. This notion of a basis document and then perfections in subsequent versions testifies to the perfection of the Constitution. Like Windows, it went through multiple iterations to get to The Constitution. Back in 1787, it was built to be the basis of the constitutional representative democracy (Republic) of the United States. If he were alive at the time, even Bill Gates would have approved.

From the National Archives:

http://www.archives.gov/national-archives-experience/charters/constitution.html

I like how this text from the national archives reads—so instead of trying to rephrase this, I simply include it below to explain the purpose of the work behind the Constitution.

The Federal Convention convened in the State House (Independence Hall) in Philadelphia on May 14, 1787, to revise the Articles of Confederation. Because the delegations from only two states were at first present, the members adjourned from day to day until a quorum of seven states was obtained on May 25. Through discussion and debate it became clear by mid-June that, rather than amend the existing Articles, the Convention would draft an entirely new frame of government.

All through the summer, in closed sessions, the delegates debated, and redrafted the articles of the new Constitution. Among the chief points at issue were how much power to allow the central government, how many representatives in Congress to allow each state, and how these representatives should be elected--directly by the people or by the state legislators. The work of many minds, the Constitution stands as a model of cooperative statesmanship and the art of compromise.

The Law of the Land

As noted previously, since 1787, the Constitution of the United States has comprised the primary law of the U.S. Federal Government. In simple terms it is the law of the land and all other laws must conform to the statutes contained within this original document and its amendments.

This law also describes the three chief branches of the Federal Government and their jurisdictions as well as the separation of the powers. It also gives the nation the ability to levy taxes, though an income tax was not permitted on people or corporations.

Ironically, there was no income tax provision in The Constitution. The Founders did not want a personal or corporate income tax mainly because it might be apportioned so that certain states paid more than others.

The people in the early twentieth century for their own reasons voted to ratify the Sixteenth amendment to the Constitution. This gave the Congress the right to tax them and US at a personal level. In the passage of this law, there was both chicanery and a lot more irony.

As hard as it may be to believe, the Sixteenth Amendment (which gave the American people the misery of confiscatory income taxes) was a trick. It never was supposed to have passed. Good people representing good people would never have permitted it.

It was introduced by the Republicans as part of a political scheme to fake-out the Democrats from a tax increase bill that would have passed but could never have been enforced because it would be unconstitutional. But, the trick backfired.

As previously noted, the Founding Fathers had rejected income taxes (as well as any other direct taxes) in the Constitution unless they were apportioned to each state according to population.

The politicians in the US Senate passed a bill to institute the Sixteenth Amendment permitting such direct taxation. The people of course would have to ratify it if it passed Congress. It surprisingly passed unanimously 77-0 in the Senate! The

House also approved it by another large margin, 318-14. Nobody was thinking!

It was then sent to the states for ratification. State after state ratified this "soak the rich" amendment, thinking it would not affect them until it went into full force and effect on February 12, 1913. The people voted to tax the rich but just about everybody has been taxed ever since. You can't outfox a foxy politician.

In the Economic Policy Journal in April 2012, David, a blogger, called it right with his opinion of many Americans. His explanation which is quoted below is that Americans would not vote for somebody, even Ron Paul who they truly believe would eliminate the income tax on everybody, because they think the rich should pay all the taxes and they should pay none. David sees it as a matter of class envy and offers a bleak outlook on the chances of it getting better until people wake up. See what he has to say:

"Americans are envious and covetous of the wealth of others. They don't want freedom. They like a government that will do things to them, so long as the resulting chains appear to be gold plated. They like politicians that stir up class envy. Humans by nature are slaves. They don't yearn to be free, responsible, independent people. Until this wholly selfish and self-centered people awakens from their slumber and learns to hate their slavery to government, until the iron of their chains eats into their soul, things are going to get worse."

The fact that Americans are beginning to get upset is a good sign. They fact that citizens such as yourself are reading a book about the Constitution is another good sign. I think this will turn around with the help of some good leaders. That means we Americans must do our best to kick every federal politician (representative) out of office and replace them with good people as soon as we can. Then we take our battle to the state capitals, and then the cities. Finally, America will be run by the people again.

Back to the Constitution

In addition to permitting all but direct taxation, The Constitution lays out the basic rights of citizens of the United States. The Constitution of the United States is the oldest federal constitution in existence in the world, and it was framed by a convention of delegates from twelve of the thirteen original states in Philadelphia in May 1787.

The Constitution is the landmark legal document of the United States and all other laws are tested against its specifications. Many other constitutions, such as the Constitution of Mexico, for example are based on this work.

The text of the entire Constitution is included in this Chapter and it is lightly referenced in Appendix E. The Bill of Rights (first ten amendments) and the other 17 amendments are shown in subsequent chapters as well as in Appendix F. Those Amendments that were submitted but not passed or ratified are shown in Appendix G.

To give the reader an appreciation or a reminder of just how significant the Articles and the Amendments of this document really are, I am including the entire text known as the Constitution in the next five chapters.

The Constitution is a free document for anybody to record and retransmit in any form. It is over two hundred twenty-five years old. It makes America, America. It is available in this book, and on the Internet from many sources and some sources are better than others.

Summary of the US Constitution

Explanation / Summary of Article I of the US Constitution:

Article I: The Legislative Branch consists of 10 sections and defines:

1. All Legislative powers,
2. Composition of the House of Representatives,
3. Composition of the Senate
4. Holding Elections,
5. Congress sets its own rules by House,
6. Compensation for Senators,
7. Revenue Bills originate in House,
8. Congress can lay and collect taxes,
9. States rights and taxes,
10. State treaties.

Note: Article I, Section 9, Clause 8 of the Constitution is of particular interest to this writer. In later chapters we lightly discuss the automatic conferring of the title, the Honorable. Please look at what the founding fathers thought of such titles:

For your convenience this is provided here and in its proper place:

Section 9 Clause 8: *No Title of Nobility shall be granted by the United States: And no Person holding any Office of Profit or Trust under them, shall, without the Consent of the Congress, accept of any present, Emolument, Office, or Title, of any kind whatever, from any King, Prince, or foreign State.*

Article II: The Executive Branch: Consists of 4 sections and defines:

(1) Executive Power and President, (2) President as Commander in Chief, (3) State of the Union & Information Requirements, (4) Rules of Executive Branch impeachment

Article III: The Judicial Branch: Consists of 3 sections and defines:

(1) Judicial Power, (2) Laws and Trial by Jury, (3) Treason

Article IV: Relations Between States: Consists of 4 sections and defines:

(1)Faith and Credit of State Laws, (2) Privileges apply to all in all states, (3) New States May be Admitted to the Union, (4) Federal guarantee to defend states.

Article V: The Amendment Process: Consists of 1 section and defines the amendment process for adding / deleting to/from the Constitution.

Article VI: General Provisions, Supremacy of the Constitution: Consists of 1 section and defines the debt process and the requirement to support the Constitution

Article VII: Ratification Process: Consists of 1 section and it outlines the process for ratifying the Constitution.

End of summary

The preamble and the detailed Articles of the US Constitution follow:

Chapter 13

The Constitution, An Awesome Document Part II of VI

Preamble through Article I Section III

The Preamble to the US Constitution:

We the People of the United States, in Order to form a more perfect Union, establish Justice, insure domestic Tranquility, provide for the common defense, promote the general Welfare, and secure the Blessings of Liberty to ourselves and our Posterity, do ordain and establish this Constitution for the United States of America.

[Explanation of the Preamble: How could the introduction to the law of the land have been written any better? The Preamble describes why the founders drafted the Constitution. It shows the desires of the Framers to improve on the government they currently had to be "more perfect" than the Articles of Confederation. The new government was to be just, and it was designed to protect citizens from internal strife and from attack from the outside. It would help the people rather be a detriment. And, perhaps as importantly, it was built to provide benefits for future generations of Americans.]

[Now, let us all look at the meat of the Constitution of the United States Of America, our country, aka—the USA! We'll begin with Article I.]

Section. I.

All legislative Powers herein granted shall be vested in a Congress of the United States, which shall consist of a Senate and House of Representatives.

[Explanation of Article I, Section I: This establishes the first of the three branches of the government, the Legislature The legislature was to be bicameral meaning two distinct chambers and it establishes the name of the legislature as *The Congress*. The Senate and the House of Representatives became the names for the two chambers.**]**

Section. II.

The House of Representatives shall be composed of Members chosen every second Year by the People of the several States, and the Electors in each State shall have the Qualifications requisite for Electors of the most numerous Branch of the State Legislature.

No Person shall be a Representative who shall not have attained to the Age of twenty five Years, and been seven Years a Citizen of the United States, and who shall not, when elected, be an Inhabitant of that State in which he shall be chosen.

Representatives and direct Taxes shall be apportioned among the several States which may be included within this Union, according to their respective Numbers, which shall be determined by adding to the whole Number of free Persons, including those bound to Service for a Term of Years, and excluding Indians not taxed, three fifths of all other Persons.

The actual Enumeration shall be made within three Years after the first Meeting of the Congress of the United States, and within every subsequent Term of ten Years, in such Manner as they shall by Law direct.

The Number of Representatives shall not exceed one for every thirty Thousand, but each State shall have at Least one Representative; and until such enumeration shall be made, the State of New Hampshire shall be entitled to choose three, Massachusetts eight, Rhode-Island and Providence Plantations one, Connecticut five, New-York six, New Jersey four, Pennsylvania eight, Delaware one, Maryland six, Virginia ten, North Carolina five, South Carolina five, and Georgia three.

When vacancies happen in the Representation from any State, the Executive Authority thereof shall issue Writs of Election to fill such Vacancies.

The House of Representatives shall choose their Speaker and other Officers; and shall have the sole Power of Impeachment.

[**Explanation of Article I, Section II:** This defines the House of Representatives, as the lower House of Congress. It also establishes several minimum requirements, such as a 25-year-old age limit. Additionally it says that the people (citizens) will elect the members of the House for two years each. The members of the House are divided among the states proportionally, aka-- according to size.

This means that the states with the larger populations are given more representatives in the House. The leader of the House is to be called The Speaker of the House, and is to be chosen by the members of the House. The number of people per representatives changed when the total become 435—nine years after the 1920 census,

The Congress at the time passed a bill called the Reapportionment Act of 1929, which set a maximum of 435 seats and established a permanent method for allocating the 435 seats in the House. Some think this move itself was unconstitutional for the Congress as they do not believe the Congress had the authority.]

Section. III.

The Senate of the United States shall be composed of two Senators from each State, chosen by the Legislature thereof for six Years; and each Senator shall have one Vote.

Immediately after they shall be assembled in Consequence of the first Election, they shall be divided as equally as may be into three Classes. The Seats of the Senators of the first Class shall be vacated at the Expiration of the second Year, of the second Class at the Expiration of the fourth Year, and of the third Class at the Expiration of the sixth Year, so that one third may be chosen every second Year; and if Vacancies happen by Resignation, or otherwise, during the Recess of the Legislature of any State, the Executive thereof may make temporary Appointments until the next Meeting of the Legislature, which shall then fill such Vacancies.

No Person shall be a Senator who shall not have attained to the Age of thirty Years, and been nine Years a Citizen of the United States, and who shall not, when elected, be an Inhabitant of that State for which he shall be chosen.

The Vice President of the United States shall be President of the Senate, but shall have no Vote, unless they be equally divided.

The Senate shall choose their other Officers, and also a President pro tempore, in the Absence of the Vice President, or when he shall exercise the Office of President of the United States.

The Senate shall have the sole Power to try all Impeachments. When sitting for that Purpose, they shall be on Oath or Affirmation. When the President of the United States is tried, the Chief Justice shall preside: And no

Person shall be convicted without the Concurrence of two thirds of the Members present.

Judgment in Cases of Impeachment shall not extend further than to removal from Office, and disqualification to hold and enjoy any Office of honor, Trust or Profit under the United States: but the Party convicted shall nevertheless be liable and subject to Indictment, Trial, Judgment and Punishment, according to Law.

{**Explanation of Article I Section III:** This defines the Senate as the upper house of Congress. It also establishes several minimum requirements, such as a 30-year-old age limit and nine years as a citizen. Senators were originally appointed by the legislatures of the individual states, though this was later changed by the Seventeenth Amendment to the Constitution, (Unlike the 435 number, this was the legitimate means of changing the Constitution).

This change permitted direct election of United States Senators by popular vote. This author thinks it was better the way the founders created it fpr today it is almost impossible for a state to recall a rogue Senator. Right after the founding the state government had the right to do so.

Additionally it says that the Senators will serve for six years each. Each state has equal suffrage in the Senate. This means that each state has the exact same number of Senators, two each, and it is not based on how small or how large a state might be in terms of the population.

In this section, the idea of a Vice-President is defined. This person, in addition to succeeding the President in the event of an emergency or death, is the President of the Senate. The Constitution provides for two officers to preside over the Senate. The Vice President of the United States is designated as the President of the Senate. A temporary president (President Pro Tempore) is also authorized. It is a high-ranking senator of the majority party who presides over the US Senate in the absence of the Vice President.

The Vice-President does not vote as a member of the US Senate unless there is a tie. He or she represents the tie breaking vote.

Many readers of the Constitution want to understand the line of succession in the event of the President's untimely death or resignation. There had been no provision for filling a vacancy in the vice presidency, and what such an appointment would mean.

When a president would die in office, the vice president would succeed him, and the vice presidency then simply remained vacant. Congress did not like the nebulous language in the Constitution re: Succession, and so they proposed the 25th amendment

This amendment supersedes the ambiguous wording of Article II, Section 1, Clause 6 of the Constitution, which does not expressly state whether the Vice President becomes the President, as opposed to an Acting President, if the President dies, resigns, is removed from office or is otherwise unable to discharge the powers of the presidency. The Twenty-fifth Amendment was adopted on February 23, 1967.

The first vice president to take office under the new procedure was Gerald Ford, who was nominated by Nixon after Spiro Agnew's resignation on Oct. 12, 1973, and confirmed by Congress the following Dec. 6, 1973.

Eight presidents have died in office. Four were assassinated and four died of natural causes. William Henry Harrison holds the dubious record for shortest term served, holding the office of presidency for 31 days before dying. Harrison was the first president to die while in office when he caught pneumonia and died on April 4, 184. Seven Vice Presidents

died in office and two resigned, John C. Calhoun and Spiro
Agnew.

The 25th Amendment solved the problem with the vice
president resigning. The Text of Section II of the 25th
Amendment is as follows:

"Whenever there is a vacancy in the office of the Vice
President, the President shall nominate a Vice President who
shall take office upon confirmation by a majority vote of both
Houses of Congress."

Please remember that it is not the names of the people but the
positions they hold that matter in terms of the line of
succession for the Presidency. The current line of succession
as of June 2016 is as follows:

- The Vice President Joseph Biden
- Speaker of the House Paul Ryan Boehner
- President pro tempore of the Senate Patrick Leahy
- Secretary of State John Kerry
- Secretary of the Treasury Jacob Lew
- Secretary of Defense Ashton Carter
- Attorney General Loretta Lynch
- Secretary of the Interior Sally Jewel
- Secretary of Agriculture Tom Vilsack
- Etc… the chain is longer…

Chapter 13

The Constitution, An Awesome Document Part III of VI

Article I Sections IV through X

Section. IV
The Times, Places and Manner of holding Elections for Senators and Representatives, shall be prescribed in each State by the Legislature thereof; but the Congress may at any time by Law make or alter such Regulations, except as to the Places of choosing Senators.

[**Explanation of Article I, Section IV:** This offers some additional requirements on the Congress. For example, the body must assemble at least once in each and every year, and the meeting shall be held on the first Monday in December, unless the Congress itself, by Law selects a different Day].

Section. V.
Each House shall be the Judge of the Elections, Returns and Qualifications of its own Members, and a Majority of each shall constitute a Quorum to do Business; but a smaller Number may adjourn from day to day, and may be authorized to compel the Attendance of absent Members, in such Manner, and under such Penalties as each House may provide.

*Each House may determine the Rules of its Proceedings,
punish its Members for disorderly Behavior, and, with the
Concurrence of two thirds, expel a Member.*

*Each House shall keep a Journal of its Proceedings, and
from time to time publish the same, excepting such Parts
as may in their Judgment require Secrecy; and the Yeas
and Nays of the Members of either House on any question
shall, at the Desire of one fifth of those Present, be entered
on the Journal.*

*Neither House, during the Session of Congress, shall,
without the Consent of the other, adjourn for more than
three days, nor to any other Place than that in which the
two Houses shall be sitting.*

[Explanation of Section V: This section demands the
following:
- — Congress must have a minimum number of
  members present in order to meet
- — Congress may set fines for members who do not
  show up.
- — Members of each House may be expelled and sent
  home with a 2/3 majority/
- — Each house must keep a journal to record
  proceedings and votes.
- — Neither house of The Congress is permitted to
  adjourn without the permission of the other.**]**

Section. VI.
*The Senators and Representatives shall receive a
Compensation for their Services, to be ascertained by Law,
and paid out of the Treasury of the United States. They
shall in all Cases, except Treason, Felony and Breach of
the Peace, be privileged from Arrest during their
Attendance at the Session of their respective Houses, and
in going to and returning from the same; and for any
Speech or Debate in either House, they shall not be
questioned in any other Place.*

No Senator or Representative shall, during the Time for which he was elected, be appointed to any civil Office under the Authority of the United States, which shall have been created, or the Emoluments whereof shall have been increased during such time; and no Person holding any Office under the United States, shall be a Member of either House during his Continuance in Office.

[Explanation of Article I, Section VI: This section establishes the following:

- All members of Congress will be paid
- Members of Congress cannot be detained while traveling to and from Congress
- Members of Congress cannot hold any other office in the government while in the Congress.**]**

Section. VII.
All Bills for raising Revenue shall originate in the House of Representatives; but the Senate may propose or concur with Amendments as on other Bills.

Every Bill which shall have passed the House of Representatives and the Senate, shall, before it become a Law, be presented to the President of the United States: If he approve he shall sign it, but if not he shall return it, with his Objections to that House in which it shall have originated, who shall enter the Objections at large on their Journal, and proceed to reconsider it.

If after such Reconsideration two thirds of that House shall agree to pass the Bill, it shall be sent, together with the Objections, to the other House, by which it shall likewise be reconsidered, and if approved by two thirds of that House, it shall become a Law. But in all such Cases the Votes of both Houses shall be determined by yeas and Nays, and the Names of the Persons voting for and against the Bill shall be entered on the Journal of each House respectively.

If any Bill shall not be returned by the President within ten Days (Sundays excepted) after it shall have been presented to him, the Same shall be a Law, in like Manner as if he had signed it, unless the Congress by their Adjournment prevent its Return, in which Case it shall not be a Law.

Every Order, Resolution, or Vote to which the Concurrence of the Senate and House of Representatives may be necessary (except on a question of Adjournment) shall be presented to the President of the United States; and before the Same shall take Effect, shall be approved by him, or being disapproved by him, shall be re-passed by two thirds of the Senate and House of Representatives, according to the Rules and Limitations prescribed in the Case of a Bill.

[Explanation of Article I Section VII: This section details how bills become law. A bill is a proposal for a new law that is introduced by a representative in the House or the Senate. It could be your representative. First, any bill for raising money (such as by taxes or fees) must start out in the House Chamber. All bills must pass both Houses of Congress in the exact same form to become law.

Bills that pass both Houses are sent to the President. He / She can either sign the bill, in which case it becomes law, or he can veto it. In the case of a veto, the bill is sent back to Congress, and if both houses pass it by a two-thirds majority, the bill becomes law over the President's veto. This is known as overriding a veto.

This section gives the President (defined in Article II) a couple more options for bills, which are presented.

The founders use the generic term he for president and so in the spirit of the founders and in the interest of brevity in this book forward, so shall this author.

First, if he neither vetoes a bill nor signs it, it becomes a law without his signature after 10 days. The second option is called a pocket veto. It occurs if Congress sends the bill to the President and they then adjourn. If the President does not sign the bill within 10 days, it does not become law.]

Section. VIII.

The Congress shall have Power To lay and collect Taxes, Duties, Imposts and Excises, to pay the Debts and provide for the common Defense and general Welfare of the United States; but all Duties, Imposts and Excises shall be uniform throughout the United States;

— *To borrow Money on the credit of the United States;*
— *To regulate Commerce with foreign Nations, and among the several States, and with the Indian Tribes;*
— *To establish an uniform Rule of Naturalization, and uniform Laws on the subject of Bankruptcies throughout the United States;*
— *To coin Money, regulate the Value thereof, and of foreign Coin, and fix the Standard of Weights and Measures;*
— *To provide for the Punishment of counterfeiting the Securities and current Coin of the United States;*
— *To establish Post Offices and post Roads;*
— *To promote the Progress of Science and useful Arts, by securing for limited Times to Authors and Inventors the exclusive Right to their respective Writings and Discoveries;*
— *To constitute Tribunals inferior to the supreme Court;*
— *To define and punish Piracies and Felonies committed on the high Seas, and Offenses against the Law of Nations;*
— *To declare War, grant Letters of Marque and Reprisal, and make Rules concerning Captures on Land and Water;*

— *To raise and support Armies, but no Appropriation of Money to that Use shall be for a longer Term than two Years;*

— *To provide and maintain a Navy;*

— *To make Rules for the Government and Regulation of the land and naval Forces;*

— *To provide for calling forth the Militia to execute the Laws of the Union, suppress Insurrections and repel Invasions;*

— *To provide for organizing, arming, and disciplining, the Militia, and for governing such Part of them as may be employed in the Service of the United States, reserving to the States respectively, the Appointment of the Officers, and the Authority of training the Militia according to the discipline prescribed by Congress;*

— *To exercise exclusive Legislation in all Cases whatsoever, over such District (not exceeding ten Miles square) as may, by Cession of particular States, and the Acceptance of Congress, become the Seat of the Government of the United States, and to exercise like Authority over all Places purchased by the Consent of the Legislature of the State in which the Same shall be, for the Erection of Forts, Magazines, Arsenals, dock-Yards, and other needful Buildings;--And*

— *To make all Laws which shall be necessary and proper for carrying into Execution the foregoing Powers, and all other Powers vested by this Constitution in the Government of the United States, or in any Department or Officer thereof.*

[**Explanation of Article I Section VIII:** This section is very readable and so no major explanation is provided. It lists the specific powers of Congress, which include the power to establish and maintain an army and navy, to establish post offices, to create courts, to regulate commerce between the states, to declare war, and to raise money. This section also includes a clause known as the Elastic Clause which allows it to pass any law necessary for the carrying out of the previously listed powers.]

Section. IX.

The Migration or Importation of such Persons as any of the States now existing shall think proper to admit, shall not be prohibited by the Congress prior to the Year one thousand eight hundred and eight, but a Tax or duty may be imposed on such Importation, not exceeding ten dollars for each Person.

The Privilege of the Writ of Habeas Corpus shall not be suspended, unless when in Cases of Rebellion or Invasion the public Safety may require it.

— *No Bill of Attainder or ex post facto* [with retroactive effect or force] *Law shall be passed.*

— *No Capitation, or other direct, Tax shall be laid, unless in Proportion to the Census or enumeration herein before directed to be taken.*

— *No Tax or Duty shall be laid on Articles exported from any State.*

— *No Preference shall be given by any Regulation of Commerce or Revenue to the Ports of one State over those of another; nor shall Vessels bound to, or from, one State, be obliged to enter, clear, or pay Duties in another.*

— *No Money shall be drawn from the Treasury, but in Consequence of Appropriations made by Law; and a regular Statement and Account of the Receipts and Expenditures of all public Money shall be published from time to time.*

— *No Title of Nobility shall be granted by the United States: And no Person holding any Office of Profit or Trust under them, shall, without the Consent of the Congress, accept of any present, Emolument, Office, or Title, of any kind whatever, from any King, Prince, or foreign State.*

[**Explanation of Article I Section IX:** In the first clause, the Constitution bars Congress from banning the importation of slaves before 1808. Until this time, as despicable as it now sounds, slaves were a commodity in the US. Still an act of Congress was necessary.

The Act of Congress which actually prohibited the importation was passed in 1807 (2 Stat. 426, enacted March 2, 1807). It is a United States federal law that stated that no new slaves were permitted to be imported into the United States. It took effect in 1808, the earliest date permitted by the United States Constitution. Unfortunately, it offered no remedy for existing slaves.

Congress cannot just willy-nilly choose to create ad hoc demands as the British Parliament appeared to do to the colonists. The colonists were not interested in going from the frying pan into the fire, and so even though it was America, they chose to place major restraints on the government so that it would be difficult for it to become tyrannical.

This section places other certain reasonable limits on Congress. Certain legal items, such as suspension of habeas corpus, bills of attainder, and ex post facto laws are prohibited. No law can give preference to one state over another; no money can be taken from the treasury except by duly passed law, and no title of nobility, such as Prince or Marquis, will ever be established by the government.]

Section. 10.

*No State shall enter into any Treaty, Alliance, or
Confederation; grant Letters of Marque and Reprisal; coin
Money; emit Bills of Credit; make any Thing but gold and
silver Coin a Tender in Payment of Debts; pass any Bill of
Attainder, ex post facto Law, or Law impairing the
Obligation of Contracts, or grant any Title of Nobility.*

*No State shall, without the Consent of the Congress, lay
any Imposts or Duties on Imports or Exports, except what
may be absolutely necessary for executing it's inspection
Laws: and the net Produce of all Duties and Imposts, laid
by any State on Imports or Exports, shall be for the Use of
the Treasury of the United States; and all such Laws shall
be subject to the Revision and Control of the Congress.*

*No State shall, without the Consent of Congress, lay any
Duty of Tonnage, keep Troops, or Ships of War in time of
Peace, enter into any Agreement or Compact with another
State, or with a foreign Power, or engage in War, unless
actually invaded, or in such imminent Danger as will not
admit of delay.*

[Explanation of Article I, Section X: At the end of Article I,
this section prohibits the states from a number of things. All
other potential restrictions not listed within the Constitution
are thereby permitted.

- The states cannot print or coin their own money
  The states cannot declare war
- The states cannot do most of the other things
  prohibited Congress to do in Section 9
- The states cannot tax goods from other states
- The states cannot have navies.

As you can see above, there is cause for amazement about
how much the colonists had a major disdain for the notion of
all royalty and nobility. As previously noted but worth bearing

a repeat, one of the first constitutional loopholes was the notion of the giver being the King, Prince, or a leader of a foreign state

There is nothing here unfortunately about taking the title ("Honorable") for oneself or having it granted via obscure rules of etiquette that have never passed the test of law. Consequently in America today, we have far too Honorables. But, from my perspective and many others, all of these titles of honor are unconstitutional because of this clause.]

Chapter 13

The Constitution, An Awesome Document Part IV of VI

Article. II. Executive Power

Section 1.

The executive Power shall be vested in a President of the United States of America. He shall hold his Office during the Term of four Years, and, together with the Vice President, chosen for the same Term, be elected, as follows:

Each State shall appoint, in such Manner as the Legislature thereof may direct, a Number of Electors, equal to the whole Number of Senators and Representatives to which the State may be entitled in the Congress: but no Senator or Representative, or Person holding an Office of Trust or Profit under the United States, shall be appointed an Elector.

The Electors shall meet in their respective States, and vote by Ballot for two Persons, of whom one at least shall not be an Inhabitant of the same State with themselves. And they shall make a List of all the Persons voted for, and of the Number of Votes for each; which List they shall sign and certify, and transmit sealed to the Seat of the Government of the United States, directed to the President of the Senate. The President of the Senate shall, in the Presence of the Senate and House of Representatives, open all the Certificates, and the Votes shall then be counted.

The Person having the greatest Number of Votes shall be the President, if such Number be a Majority of the whole Number of Electors appointed; and if there be more than one who have such Majority, and have an equal Number of Votes, then the House of Representatives shall immediately chuse by Ballot one of them for President; and if no Person have a Majority, then from the five highest on the List the said House shall in like Manner choose the President.

But in choosing the President, the Votes shall be taken by States, the Representation from each State having one Vote; A quorum for this purpose shall consist of a Member or Members from two thirds of the States, and a Majority of all the States shall be necessary to a Choice. In every Case, after the Choice of the President, the Person having the greatest Number of Votes of the Electors shall be the Vice President. But if there should remain two or more who have equal Votes, the Senate shall choose from them by Ballot the Vice President.

The Congress may determine the Time of choosing the Electors, and the Day on which they shall give their Votes; which Day shall be the same throughout the United States.

No Person except a natural born Citizen, or a Citizen of the United States, at the time of the Adoption of this Constitution, shall be eligible to the Office of President; neither shall any Person be eligible to that Office who shall not have attained to the Age of thirty five Years, and been fourteen Years a Resident within the United States.

In Case of the Removal of the President from Office, or of his Death, Resignation, or Inability to discharge the Powers and Duties of the said Office, the Same shall devolve on the Vice President, and the Congress may by Law provide for the Case of Removal, Death, Resignation or Inability, both of the President and Vice President, declaring what Officer shall then act as President, and such Officer shall act accordingly, until the Disability be removed, or a President shall be elected.

The President shall, at stated Times, receive for his Services, a Compensation, which shall neither be increased nor diminished during the Period for which he shall have been elected, and he shall not receive within that Period any other Emolument from the United States, or any of them.

Before he enter on the Execution of his Office, he shall take the following Oath or Affirmation:--"I do solemnly swear (or affirm) that I will faithfully execute the Office of President of the United States, and will to the best of my Ability, preserve, protect and defend the Constitution of the United States."

[**Explanation of Article II Section I:** The purpose of Article II is to establish the second of the three branches of government, the Executive Branch. The Legislative Branch (House & Senate) were defined in Article I. Section 1 establishes the office of the President and the Vice-President. It sets their terms to be four years for each of them.

Presidents are not elected by the people per se. Instead, there is this notion called the Electoral College, and they elect the President. The people have a big say in the matter as they vote for Electoral College delegates who then vote for the President according to their state's wishes. Each state has one vote in the "Electoral College" for each member of Congress.

Originally, the President was the person with the most votes and the Vice-President was the person with the second most, though this was later changed to recognize that a Democrat President should have a Democrat VP. This was not always the case.

When John Adams became President, he was a member of the long-gone Federalist Party. Thomas Pinckney was his running mate. He was a Democratic-Republican, a party whose name has also disappeared.

Aaron Burr, was Jefferson's running mate in the election of 1796. Despite being from different parties, Adams and Jefferson were the President and Vice-President respectively for four years. After Adams, the next highest vote getter was Thomas Jefferson. The twelfth Amendment made it so both the President and Vice-President heretofore would be from the same political party even if it were the Rathskellar Party or the Liquor Party!

In Article II, Section I, other minimum requirements were established again, such as a 35-year minimum age. Presidents must also be natural-born citizens of the United States. The President is to be paid a salary, which cannot change, up or down, as long as he is in office.]

Section. II.
The President shall be Commander in Chief of the Army and Navy of the United States, and of the Militia of the several States, when called into the actual Service of the United States; he may require the Opinion, in writing, of the principal Officer in each of the executive Departments, upon any Subject relating to the Duties of their respective Offices, and he shall have Power to grant Reprieves and Pardons for Offences against the United States, except in Cases of Impeachment.

He shall have Power, by and with the Advice and Consent of the Senate, to make Treaties, provided two thirds of the Senators present concur; and he shall nominate, and by and with the Advice and Consent of the Senate, shall appoint Ambassadors, other public Ministers and Consuls, Judges of the supreme Court, and all other Officers of the United States, whose Appointments are not herein otherwise provided for, and which shall be established by

Law: but the Congress may by Law vest the Appointment of such inferior Officers, as they think proper, in the President alone, in the Courts of Law, or in the Heads of Departments.

The President shall have Power to fill up all Vacancies that may happen during the Recess of the Senate, by granting Commissions which shall expire at the End of their next Session.

[Explanation of Article II Section II: This provides the President some important powers. He is the top commander-in-chief of the armed forces and of the militia (National Guard) of all the states; he has a Cabinet of people in various capacities such as war and education to assist him, and he has the power to pardon criminals.

The President makes treaties with other nations, and he picks many of the judges and other members of the government (all must be with the expressed approval of the US Senate). The founders did not trust that any man or body of men and/or women could be trusted over time without major restraints. The Constitution is the basis for those restraints.

And, in the twenty-first century in which we live, when citizens observe the government doing its own thing rather than abiding by the Constitution, there is a rightful call to alarm.]

Section. III.
He shall from time to time give to the Congress Information of the State of the Union, and recommend to their Consideration such Measures as he shall judge necessary and expedient; he may, on extraordinary Occasions, convene both Houses, or either of them, and in Case of Disagreement between them, with Respect to the Time of Adjournment, he may adjourn them to such Time as he shall think proper; he shall receive Ambassadors and other public Ministers; he shall take Care that the Laws be

faithfully executed, and shall Commission all the Officers of the United States.

[Explanation of Article II, Section III: This section delineates the duties of the President:
— To give a state of the union address.
— To make suggestions to Congress.
— To act as head of state by receiving ambassadors and other heads of state.
— To assure that the laws of the United-States are carried out.
—

Americans paying attention have noticed that the current president has decided that he does not need to carry out laws of which he does not agree. Clearly as you observe the creed set forth in this section, you will note that no President has such authority. Thus, many suggest we are in a state of tyranny today.]

Section. IV.
The President, Vice President and all civil Officers of the United States, shall be removed from Office on Impeachment for, and Conviction of, Treason, Bribery, or other high Crimes and Misdemeanors.

[Explanation of Article II Section IV: This section briefly discusses the notion of removing a President from office in a process known as impeachment. Perhaps if this notion were better clarified by the framers, in recent years when impeachment has been desirable, it might even be able to be effected without the concurrence of both or the many as it may be, political parties in standing.]

Chapter 13

The Constitution, An Awesome Document Part V of VI

Article III. Establishes Supreme Court and other courts

Section. I.

The judicial Power of the United States shall be vested in one supreme Court, and in such inferior Courts as the Congress may from time to time ordain and establish. The Judges, both of the supreme and inferior Courts, shall hold their Offices during good Behavior, and shall, at stated Times, receive for their Services a Compensation, which shall not be diminished during their Continuance in Office.

[**Explanation of Article III Section I:** This establishes the last of the three branches of government, the Judiciary. In this section, the Supreme Court is established. This is the highest court in the United States. It also sets the terms of all federal judges, of both the Supreme Court and lower courts: that they serve as long as they are on "good behavior," which usually means for life (No Justice and only a few judges have ever been impeached). State judges typically are voted in for specific terms. This section also requires that federal judges shall be paid for their work.]

Section. II

The judicial Power shall extend to all Cases, in Law and Equity, arising under this Constitution, the Laws of the United States, and Treaties made, or which shall be made, under their Authority;--to all Cases affecting Ambassadors, other public Ministers and Consuls;--to all Cases of admiralty and maritime Jurisdiction;--to Controversies to which the United States shall be a Party;--to Controversies between two or more States;-- between a State and Citizens of another State;--between Citizens of different States;--between Citizens of the same State claiming Lands under Grants of different States, and between a State, or the Citizens thereof, and foreign States, Citizens or Subjects.

In all Cases affecting Ambassadors, other public Ministers and Consuls, and those in which a State shall be Party, the supreme Court shall have original Jurisdiction. In all the other Cases before mentioned, the supreme Court shall have appellate Jurisdiction, both as to Law and Fact, with such Exceptions, and under such Regulations as the Congress shall make.

The Trial of all Crimes, except in Cases of Impeachment, shall be by Jury; and such Trial shall be held in the State where the said Crimes shall have been committed; but when not committed within any State, the Trial shall be at such Place or Places as the Congress may by Law have directed.

[Explanation of Article III Section II: This section sets a number of important things for the federal judiciary:

— The types of cases that may be heard,
— Which cases the Supreme Court may hear first (called original jurisdiction),
— All other cases heard by the Supreme Court are by appeal.
— It also guarantees trial by jury in criminal court.]

Section. III.
Treason against the United States, shall consist only in levying War against them, or in adhering to their Enemies,

giving them Aid and Comfort. No Person shall be convicted of Treason unless on the Testimony of two Witnesses to the same overt Act, or on Confession in open Court.

The Congress shall have Power to declare the Punishment of Treason, but no Attainder of Treason shall work Corruption of Blood, or Forfeiture except during the Life of the Person attainted.

[**Explanation of Article III, Section III:** This section defines the crime of treason against the United States. Treason is the only crime specifically defined in the Constitution. A person is engaged in treason if he or she goes to war against the United States or gives "aid or comfort" to an enemy. This is self-evident. However, he or she does not have to use a weapon and fight in combat against U.S. forces. Treasonous acts include helping the enemy by passing along classified information or supplying weapons or knowledge of critical war locations and positions.

Protesting or demonstrating for or against a war is not a treasonous act and in fact is protected by the free speech clause in the First Amendment. To be convicted of treason, a supposed perpetrator must either admit guilt in open court or be implicated by the testimony of two witnesses.

Attainder brings dishonor for it is the legal consequence of judgment of death or outlawry for treason or felony. It involves the loss of all civil rights. A bill of attainder in English law was a legislative act that singled out one or more persons and imposed punishment on them, without benefit of a judicial trial. The Constitution forbids this. In the case of treason, the crimes of the father may result in punishment to the son. Thus, The Congress may set the punishment, but it must be directed only at the guilty person and not at his or her friends or family if they were not involved in the crime.]

Article. IV. Regarding the states

Section. I.
Full Faith and Credit shall be given in each State to the public Acts, Records, and judicial Proceedings of every other State. And the Congress may by general Laws prescribe the Manner in which such Acts, Records and Proceedings shall be proved, and the Effect thereof.

[**Explanation of Article IV, Section I:** This section mandates that all states must honor the laws of all other states. The purpose of this, for example is that if a couple married under the laws of the nation and of say Florida is also considered married by Arizona, or that someone convicted of a crime in Virginia is considered guilty in Wyoming. There has been some confusion regarding this section regarding some of the new issues regarding marriage within American society.]

Section. II.
The Citizens of each State shall be entitled to all Privileges and Immunities of Citizens in the several States.

A Person charged in any State with Treason, Felony, or other Crime, who shall flee from Justice, and be found in another State, shall on Demand of the executive Authority of the State from which he fled, be delivered up, to be removed to the State having Jurisdiction of the Crime.

No Person held to Service or Labor in one State, under the Laws thereof, escaping into another, shall, in Consequence of any Law or Regulation therein, be discharged from such Service or Labor, but shall be delivered up on Claim of the Party to whom such Service or Labor may be due.

[**Explanation of Article IV Section II:** This section guarantees that citizens of one state be treated equally and fairly like all citizens of another state. If a person, who is accused of a crime in one state, flees to another, this section requires that the potential criminal be returned to the state from which they fled. Additionally, this section offers a remedy for handling fugitive slaves, which no longer applies, as slavery has not been permitted in the US since April 1864 with the passage of the Thirteenth Amendment to the Constitution.]

Section. III.

New States may be admitted by the Congress into this Union; but no new State shall be formed or erected within the Jurisdiction of any other State; nor any State be formed by the Junction of two or more States, or Parts of States, without the Consent of the Legislatures of the States concerned as well as of the Congress.

The Congress shall have Power to dispose of and make all needful Rules and Regulations respecting the Territory or other Property belonging to the United States; and nothing in this Constitution shall be so construed as to Prejudice any Claims of the United States, or of any particular State.

[**Explanation of Article IV Section III:** This section concerns the admittance of new states and the control of federal lands. Congress can admit new states into the Union, but a single state cannot create a new state within its boundaries. For example, the state of New Hampshire cannot make Berlin, NH a separate state. Likewise two states cannot merge to be one state.

There are lands that are controlled by the United States that are not states—such as Washington D.C., and Puerto Rico. This section provides the US the right to set rules for any of lands owned by the United States, such as the national parks and national forests. There is a lot of opportunity for misunderstanding regarding lands theoretically owned by the federal government which they have been by law required to give back but have not. Cliven Bundy and Nevada is a recent example.

Section. IV.

The United States shall guarantee to every State in this Union a Republican Form of Government, and shall protect each of them against Invasion; and on Application of the Legislature, or of the Executive (when the Legislature cannot be convened), against domestic Violence.

[**Explanation for Article IV Section IV:** This section prescribes republican form of government (which, in this case, is synonymous with "Constitutional representative democracy—not a monarchy, oligarchy, or any aristocratic scheme). The country derives its power from the people, not from a king or emperor. This guarantees that the federal government will protect all the states against invasion and insurrection—even if the President does not like that particular state.]

Chapter 13 Part VI of VI

The Constitution, An Awesome Document Part VI of VI

Articles V through VII

Article. V. Changing the Constitution in the future

The Congress, whenever two thirds of both Houses shall deem it necessary, shall propose Amendments to this Constitution, or, on the Application of the Legislatures of two thirds of the several States, shall call a Convention for proposing Amendments, which, in either Case, shall be valid to all Intents and Purposes, as Part of this Constitution, when ratified by the Legislatures of three fourths of the several States, or by Conventions in three fourths thereof, as the one or the other Mode of Ratification may be proposed by the Congress; Provided that no Amendment which may be made prior to the Year One thousand eight hundred and eight shall in any Manner affect the first and fourth Clauses in the Ninth Section of the first Article; and that no State, without its Consent, shall be deprived of its equal Suffrage in the Senate.

[**Explanation of Article V:** The Constitution can only be modified / amended by the specific method provided in Article V. The framers realized that over time, things would need to be spelled out better or the country's mood on certain issues would change and the nation needed a way to change the Constitution to meet such specific needs in a non-frivolous manner. And, so, the Constitution is very difficult to change, and this is good for the nation.

No act of Congress or Executive Order or Court Order can change the Constitution. The process to change the Constitution involves two thirds of the members of Congress proposing specific amendments; or they may call a convention in which amendments to the Constitution can be put forth. No amendment becomes part of the Constitution unless three fourths of the total # of states in the Union ratify (approve) the amendment(s) in their own state legislatures. When proposed, passed, and ratified, an amendment becomes a permanent change to the Constitution.

The President has no authority to ignore any Constitutional Amendment. To make sure that all was on the up and up, the framers wrote so that three specific amendments were forbidden:

- To deny a state its votes in the Senate,
- That before 1808 would enable Congress to prohibit the importation of slaves
- That before 1808 would allow direct taxation except as based on the system of enumeration set out in Article I, Section 2.

As a result, the framers of the Constitution created a three-fifths compromise contained in Article I, Section 9, for how, slaves would be counted when determining a state's total population for constitutional purposes. This remained in place until 1808 when Congress banned the international slave trade.]

Article. VI. **Regarding the United States itself**

All Debts contracted and Engagements entered into, before the Adoption of this Constitution, shall be as valid against the United States under this Constitution, as under the Confederation.

This Constitution, and the Laws of the United States which shall be made in Pursuance thereof; and all Treaties made, or which shall be made, under the Authority of the United States, shall be the supreme Law of the Land; and the Judges in every State shall be bound thereby, any Thing in the Constitution or Laws of any State to the Contrary notwithstanding.

The Senators and Representatives before mentioned, and the Members of the several State Legislatures, and all executive and judicial Officers, both of the United States and of the several States, shall be bound by Oath or Affirmation, to support this Constitution; but no religious Test shall ever be required as a Qualification to any Office or public Trust under the United States.

Explanation of Article VI: This concerns the United States itself.

1. It guarantees that the United States under the Constitution would assume all debts and contracts entered into by the United States under the Articles of Confederation.
2. It sets the Constitution and all laws and treaties of the United States to be the supreme law of the country.
3. It requires all officers of the United States and of the states to swear an oath of allegiance to the United States and the Constitution when taking office.]

Article. VII.

The Ratification of the Conventions of nine States shall be sufficient for the Establishment of this Constitution between the States so ratifying the Same.

[Explanation of Article VII: This Article details the method for ratification, or acceptance, of the Constitution: of the original 13 states in the United States. Nine states had to accept the Constitution before it would officially go into effect.]

Framers notes at the end of the Constitution:

The Word, "the," being interlined between the seventh and eighth Lines of the first Page, the Word "Thirty" being partly written on an Erazure in the fifteenth Line of the first Page, The Words "is tried" being interlined between the thirty second and thirty third Lines of the first Page and the Word "the" being interlined between the forty third and forty fourth Lines of the second Page.

Attest William Jackson Secretary

Closing clause of the US Constitution

Done in Convention by the Unanimous Consent of the States present the Seventeenth Day of September in the Year of our Lord one thousand seven hundred and Eighty seven and of the Independence of the United States of America the Twelfth In witness whereof We have hereunto subscribed our Names,

George Washington

President and Deputy from Virginia

Delaware
Geo Read, Gunning Bedford, John Dickinson, Richard Bassett, Jaco Broom

Maryland
James McHenry, Dan of St Thos. Jenifer Daniel Carroll

Virginia
John Blair, James Madison Jr.

North Carolina
William Blount, Richard Dobbs Spaight, Hume Williamson

South Carolina
J. Rutledge, Charles Cotesworth Pinckney, Charles Pinckney, Pierce Butler

Georgia
William Few, Abraham Baldwin

New Hampshire
John Langdon, Nicholas Gilman,

Massachusetts
Nathaniel Gorham, Rufus King

Connecticut
William. Samuel Johnson, Roger Sherman

New York
Alexander Hamilton,

New Jersey
William Livingston, David Brearley, William Paterson, Jonathan Dayton

Pennsylvania
Ben Franklin, Thomas Mifflin, Robert. Morris, George. Clymer, Thomas. FitzSimons, Jared Ingersoll, James Wilson, Gouv Morris

Rhode Island and its provinces were not represented. New Yourk's representatives left before the convention had created the Constitution.

Reference with spelling corrections:
http://www.archives.gov/national-archives-experience/charters/constitution_transcript.html

Part V Patriotic Documents Post Constitution

Chapter 14

The Bill of Rights Part I of II

The fight over the Bill of Rights

Now, that you and I have exhaustingly traversed multiple chapters, some with multiple parts, throughout this book in search of the perfect constitution, should we believe that we have found it? I say yes! It is The Constitution of the United States of America. In its own rules, it prescribes a way for it to be changed, as long as the people agree. Who can ask for anything more?

It offers no opportunity for the congress or the president to choose to act other than directed by the Constitution and the laws enacted by Congress. In the terms of the forty-fourth President, there are a number of accusations of lawlessness.

The laws broken include the Constitution and other laws enacted by Congress, which the current President has sworn to enforce. The current President has no problem with calling a weak Congress's bluff and so he reigns, un-impeached. However, more and more citizens are finding the lawlessness of the Executive Branch a little too much to handle, and are demanding Congress to act to assure the Constitution.

The Constitution, though a phenomenal instrument of government for America, is not 100% perfect. As I like to say in its defense, it is more perfect than any other supreme body of law in any other country, including Bimini, which is a beautiful island in the Bahamas.

If this were not so, you, I would be seeking refuge in Bimini, or the next most free country in the world. Right now, because of our Constitution, we would find the country that provides full freedom and liberty in all cases to be the United States of America. There is no expiration date on the United States.

Americans paying attention know that the best set of laws for both the hoi polloi (regular people) and the hoity-toity (the elite among us) is our one of a kind US Constitution.

So why, with such a fine Constitution is a separate "Bill of Rights" required? If the Constitution is almost perfect, why was it not enough? Why is it not enough? "Why did we ever need a Bill of Rights?

In this modern era, where all traditional values are questioned, there is a film and a video game known as the Bill of Rights. Both media notions (film & video game) attempt to tell the story about a struggle among the Founders and the Framers of the US Constitution that nearly tore the nation apart.

It was even before the US had a Constitution to assure its future. Toward the end of the 16 minute documentary, the Bill of Rights is described as "absolutely essential to our national character."

When the Founders were founding the nation, there was no notion of political parties, and that is why the brave men of those times were able to come together to delineate a set of laws that would be able to guide America forever. Even then, of course there was the risk of a scoundrel in an important office, and that scoundrel, even if he were the President, might choose to ignore the laws of the past.

Therefore, the folks at that time, some who believed the Constitution was perfect, and others who thought that our rights needed to be declared outwardly in a positive sense, needed to come together.

The Constitution gave the people all the power but to be fair, the specific rights were not delineated. And, so an errant judge in the future, wrong as he or she might be, could decree that there is no right in the Constitution guaranteeing you freedom of speech. Then what?

The Bill of rights therefore specifically, forcefully, and more authoritatively defines the rights of the people. Some people in 1787 had a major issue about whether the US Constitution restricted government powers enough to assure that Americans had perpetual liberty under the law. Today's people can understand why!

If Government had no power to restrict the power of the people, then why should the people need a specific bill of rights? The simple answer is that after hundreds of years of tyranny in their home countries, the colonists trusted nobody, and they therefore recognized the possibility of an errant judge in the future misunderstanding the Constitution.

The framers of The Constitution gave no rights to government other than those so enumerated specifically in the Constitution. There were few of these. So, many of the framers did not believe that the people needed a bill of rights since government could theoretically never take away the inalienable rights the people already possessed.

The Constitution gave the government no power to override the will of the people. Others were concerned that since people are people, scoundrels might emerge as leaders and the

people would have no backup column to present to prove
their rights. They looked for a specific Bill of Rights!

Implication or Specification?

The battle of whether a Bill of Rights was necessary during the
founding and framing of the Constitution is a matter of
implication or specification. Those who believed the
government was sufficiently verboten from taking away
individual liberty saw no reason to specify (specification) the
liberties that could not be taken away. Their answer was "no
liberties" can be taken from the people. Implicit or explicit,
when quoted, we all like to have an explicit quote upon which
to base our contention.

Well, the explicits and the implicits got their day of discussion
and they worked for the good of all to come up with
something that would work. Out of their compromise came
one of our nation's most central documents and the
foundation for some of our most celebrated obvious freedoms.
The document produced to represent their thoughts is forever
known as the Bill of Rights.

Whether it was needed logically or not needed logically, it is
the Bill of Rights that guaranteed the ratification of The
Constitution. It was enough to convince the patriots that the
Constitution was to be approved. Americans wanted written
assurance that the rights they fought for as colonists against
Britain in the American Revolution would not be taken away.
They believed their rights should be protected by a written
document. The Bill of Rights served that purpose.

Without the Bill of Rights, some of the states refused to ratify
The Constitution since at first cut, a national Bill of Rights
was not included. Thus the Bill of Rights was an essential
ingredient to having a Constitution pass the states.

Without the *Bill of Rights* we would have never been able to
ratify the Constitution that brought more stability to our

nation. The Constitution and the specifics in the *Bill of Rights* and the other seventeen Amendments have helped our country survive during the times of instability and confusion concerning how to properly organize and run the nation.

The *Bill of Rights* was carved out after the Constitution had been written. And, though it is deemed by many to be an integral "part" of the Constitution, when offered to the people, it was created independently of the Constitution and presented as an add-on.

The *Bill of Rights* indeed is the first ten ratified / approved amendments to the US Constitution. The original framers trusted that we would never turn on the precepts in the Constitution. Those insisting on the need for a Bill of Rights wanted to assure themselves that we could not even find a loophole to limit our rights.

We all know by now that the Constitution guarantees every American certain basic rights including: freedom of speech, freedom of religion, the right to assembly, the right to a jury trial, etc. These are just some of the rights implicitly protected by our Constitution. But these freedoms, though implicit, were not explicitly stated in the original version of the Constitution. It took the *Bill of Rights* to mention them explicitly.

You have already read the full Constitution in this book. You know nothing was written to implicitly or specifically grant the freedoms in the Bill of Rights to all Americans. In fact, as noted, many of the framers of the Constitution were dead set against including such a Bill in the document even as amendments.

The Framers were very smart people. They knew that when they had written the Constitution, they had implicitly granted all those provisions in the Bill of Rights simply by denying government such rights. In truth, implicit provisions are far more powerful and long-serving than those explicitly provided.

But, honest regular people at the time, looking for truth have a tough time understanding implicit notions. And, so the explicit provisions of the Bill of Rights helped many Americans, who did not profess to be Constitutional scholars to lean towards the ratification of the Constitution with ten rights explicitly noted.

Thus, as the debate ensued, the non-trusting were compelled by their very nature to demand as many explicit provisions from the new government as possible. The colonists did not trust any government at the time.

As we all know, humans have limited attention spans. Worse than that, historical governments have most often gone bad over time. So, why would the regular folks in America back those wanting votes for the Constitution without "proper" guarantees for liberty and freedom over time?

And, so a look back does say that a Bill of Rights needed to be created and added to the Constitution. James Madison, one of the major authors of the Federalist Papers, and a great patriot, who eventually became the fourth President of the United States was enlisted to write many of the precepts in the Bill of Rights. Like Alexander Hamilton, he was a phenomenal author. He is credited with being the primary author of the Constitution and so he is known by historians as the "Father of the Constitution."

Ironically, Madison did not think a Bill of Rights was necessary. He took issue, though lightly, with those who felt that the Constitution should grant rights. Instead, he felt that the people had all the rights, according to the Constitution and the government had no rights other than those explicitly granted by the people.

Consequently Madison would have been against any Bill of Rights and the document that emerged from the Constitutional Convention in 1787 reflected his conviction. He believed the Constitution as it was written already spelled out what the Federal Government could do and not do. He believed that if it wasn't in that document, it wasn't any of the Federal Government's business. No further protection was necessary.

Of course James Madison never met a 20th or 21st Century leftist politician looking for an excuse to break through the limitations on government provided in the Constitution to further the cause of communism. These scoundrels love their rights yet want the rights of others taken away to suit their interests. Some think that the Bill of Rights has only postponed the villains, who outwardly shows disdain for the freedoms granted to Americans by the Constitution.

As recently as late May 2014, for example, the current President at the time challenged the notion of Article II regarding two Senators from each state. The President said it is unfair that hugely populated Democratic States such as New York and California get just two Senators when they have lots more people. If you are reading this book in 2067, it would save some research for you to know that the current President, who presides while I am writing this book, is a leftist long before he is an American.

Will this President, with lack of any deep love for America and the Constitution, try by Executive Order to change the Constitution? Readers in 2014 already know the answer.

He has already done this with other laws such as those pertaining to immigration and social issues. This, of course is why his administration is considered lawless. It helps to remember that many colonists were concerned that a strong national government was a threat to individual rights and that the President might become a king, and that strengthened their demand for more explicit rights. .

Therefore, to most conservative Americans it is better to explicitly state rights than to have a politician motivated by political opportunism take matters into their own hands.

George Mason, a Virginia delegate vigorously disagreed with James Madison. He was not so sure that the new government would provide anything better than the rights the British provided, and then took back when it was convenient.

Despite being wounded in spirit and in the wallet, Americans in the eighteenth century all knew that a long and bloody war to win independence had only recently ended. Though Madison et al believed they had protected Americans in the text of The Constitution, Mason and others wanted to explicitly ensure that the new government could not erase the freedoms the Patriots had fought so hard to secure.

George Mason declared that he would rather "chop off my right hand" than support a Constitution that did not include a Bill of Rights.

If we are looking for forefathers of things like Articles and Declarations and Constitutions, we might well credit George Mason as the Father of the Bill of Rights.

Depending on your level of trust in the positive precepts of the Constitution as originally written, it is reasonable to believe that the more assurances of freedom the better. Those patriots looking for more assurances won and The Bill of Rights was added to the Constitution as the first ten amendments on December 15, 1791.

The fact that the Constitution did not include a Bill of Rights to specifically protect Americans' hard-won rights had certainly sparked the most heated debates during the

ratification process. Now that we know there is such a Bill;
what rights do they give?

Let's go over a few for a second or third time as all of us have
a tendency to forget important things until we realize how
important they really are.

As previously noted, the Bill of Rights are the first ten
amendments (changes) to the United States Constitution.
Madison saw no real problem with the Bill of Rights other
than their redundancy for he already believed they existed
implicitly within the Constitution.

Rather than risk destroying the Constitution, Jefferson, out of
town during the debate, wrote to Madison advocating a Bill of
Rights: "Half a loaf is better than no bread. If we cannot
secure all our rights, let us secure what we can." So, Madison
introduced the Bill of Rights as a series of amendments on
June 8, 1789 in the First Federal Congress.

Who wrote the Bill of Rights? George Mason, who would not
sign the Constitution without the Bill of Rights and James
Madison, who felt they were not needed, are considered by
historians to be among the two primary authors of the twelve
articles in the original Bill of Rights.

Ten of the amendments of the twelve were ratified without
much debate and they became the Bill of Rights in 1791.
These amendments specify rights of citizens explicitly by their
content and implicitly by "further" limiting the powers of the
federal government. They protect the rights of all citizens,
residents and visitors on United States territory. More people
today understand the Bill of Rights than those that understand
the full impact of the US Constitution.

In this book about the US Constitution, it is most appropriate,
for sure to include this discussion of the first ten ratified

amendments to the US Constitution known as the Bill of
Rights.

About the Bill of Rights?

So, what is meant by the term Bill of Rights? It represents the
full notion of the first ten amendments to the United States
Constitution. Amendments are supposed to be changes even
though Madison believed these ten Amendments, and the
rights they gave American citizens existed implicitly in the
original drafting of the US Constitution. Madison saw the Bill
as being redundant; but redundancy on a topic such as liberty
and freedom was OK with him. In the end, Madison was OK
with the Bill of Rights.

These amendments, known as the Bill of Rights were specific
rights to be granted to citizens even if they had not conceived
they already had the rights simply because the Constitution
granted no such rights to government. The Bill of Rights in
summary explicitly limits the Federal government's powers,
protects the rights of the people by preventing Congress from
abridging freedom of speech, freedom of the press, freedom of
assembly, freedom of religious worship, and the right to bear
arms, and many others rights as noted in ten specific
amendments.

For example, the Bill of Rights prevents unreasonable search
and seizure, cruel and unusual punishment, and self-
incrimination, and it guarantees due process of law and a
speedy public trial with an impartial jury.

In addition, the Bill of Rights states that "the enumeration in
the Constitution, of certain rights, shall not be construed to
deny or disparage others (rights) retained by the people," and
reserves all powers not specifically granted to the Federal
government to the citizenry or States. The original Ten
Amendments to the Constitution, The Bill of Rights was
introduced by Madison and passed by Congress September

25, 1789. These amendments came into effect when three/fourths of the states ratified them on December 15, 1791—four years after the Constitution had been created.

Chapter 14

The Bill of Rights Part II of II

Text of the Bill of Rights

The Bill of Rights is seen as the third of the three charters of freedom—the pillars of our Republic. Along with the Declaration of Independence and the Constitution, the Bill of Rights defines America. The Bill was granted by the Congress of the United States, begun and held at the City of New-York, on Wednesday the fourth of March, one thousand seven hundred and eighty nine.

The text of the Bill looks exactly as follows:

THE Conventions of a number of the States, having at the time of their adopting the Constitution, expressed a desire, in order to prevent misconstruction or abuse of its powers, that further declaratory and restrictive clauses should be added; And as extending the ground of public confidence in the Government, will best ensure the beneficent ends of its institution.

RESOLVED by the Senate and House of Representatives of the United States of America, in Congress assembled, two thirds of both Houses concurring, that the following Articles be proposed to the Legislatures of the several States, as amendments to the Constitution of the United States, all, or any of which Articles, when ratified by three-fourths of the said

Legislatures, to be valid to all intents and purposes, as part of the said Constitution; viz.

ARTICLES in addition to, and Amendment of the Constitution of the United States of America, proposed by Congress, and ratified by the Legislatures of the several States, pursuant to the fifth Article of the original Constitution.

Article the first. ... After the first enumeration required by the first article of the Constitution, there shall be one Representative for every 30,000 until the number shall amount to 100, after which the proportion shall be so regulated by Congress, that there shall be not less than 100 Representatives, nor less than one Representative for every 40,000 persons, until the number of Representatives shall amount to 200; after which the proportion shall be so regulated by Congress, that there shall not be less than 200 Representatives, nor more than one Representative for every 50,000 persons.

Article the second ... No law, varying the compensation for the services of the Senators and Representatives, shall take effect, until an election of Representatives shall have intervened.

Article the third ... Congress shall make no law respecting an establishment of religion, or prohibiting the free exercise thereof; or abridging the freedom of speech, or of the press; or the right of the people peaceably to assemble, and to petition the Government for a redress of grievances.

Article the fourth ... A well regulated Militia, being necessary to the security of a free state, the right of the people to keep and bear arms, shall not be infringed.

Article the fifth ... No soldier shall, in time of peace be quartered in any house, without the consent of the owner, nor in time of war, but in a manner to be prescribed by law.

Article the sixth ... *The right of the people to be secure in their persons, houses, papers, and effects, against unreasonable searches and seizures, shall not be violated, and no Warrants shall issue, but upon probable cause, supported by Oath or affirmation, and particularly describing the place to be searched, and the persons or things to be seized.*

Article the seventh ... *No person shall be held to answer for a capital, or otherwise infamous crime, unless on a presentment or indictment of a Grand Jury, except in cases arising in the land or naval forces, or in the Militia, when in actual service in time of war or public danger; nor shall any person be subject for the same offence to be twice put in jeopardy of life or limb; nor shall be compelled in any criminal case to be a witness against himself, nor be deprived of life, liberty, or property, without due process of law; nor shall private property be taken for public use, without just compensation.*

Article the eighth ... *In all criminal prosecutions, the accused shall enjoy the right to a speedy and public trial, by an impartial jury of the State and district wherein the crime shall have been committed, which district shall have been previously ascertained by law, and to be informed of the nature and cause of the accusation; to be confronted with the witnesses against him; to have compulsory process for obtaining witnesses in his favor, and to have the Assistance of Counsel for his defense.*

Article the ninth ... *In suits at common law, where the value in controversy shall exceed twenty dollars, the right of trial by jury shall be preserved, and no fact tried by a jury, shall be otherwise re-examined in any Court of the United States, than according to the rules of the common law.*

Article the tenth *... Excessive bail shall not be required, nor excessive fines imposed, nor cruel and unusual punishments inflicted.*

Article the eleventh *.... The enumeration in the Constitution, of certain rights, shall not be construed to deny or disparage others retained by the people.*

Article the twelfth *... The powers not delegated to the United States by the Constitution, nor prohibited by it to the States, are reserved to the States respectively, or to the people."*

ATTEST,

Frederick Augustus Muhlenberg Speaker of the House of Representatives

John Adams, Vice-President of the United States, and President of the Senate.

John Beckley, Clerk of the House of Representatives. Sam A. Otis, Secretary of the Senate.

This work is in the public domain in the United States because it is a work of the United States

One more fact on the Bill of Rights is essential. The "Bill of Rights" is actually the popular name for a joint resolution passed by the first U.S. Congress on September 25, 1789.

The resolution proposed the first set of twelve amendments to the Constitution. Then as now, the process of amending the Constitution required that the resolution be "ratified" or approved by at least three quarters of the states. Unlike the 10 amendments we know and cherish today as the Bill of Rights, the resolution sent to the states for ratification in 1789, proposed twelve amendments, not just ten. Knowing the body of law known as the Bill of Rights consists of just ten amendments, we therefore know that two were not ratified.

When the votes came in, from the 11 states that participated, on December 15, 1791, only the last 10 of the 12 amendments submitted had been ratified. And, so as you scour the original amendments looking for familiar text as in the First Amendment, you will have to cast your eyes to the third amendment proposed to find the contents of the first amendment as ratified.

Thus, the original third amendment, establishing freedom of speech, press, assembly, petition, and the right to a fair and speedy trial became today's First Amendment. Yet, when proposed, it was the third amendment.

The First Ten Constitutional Amendments

Depending on one's purpose when they write there is often permitted an amount of redundancy, especially if the writing is for educational purposes. Most people upon hearing something once, unless it is particularly interesting or particularly wonderful, or particularly grievous, are inclined to forget it. And, so, you may have already detected the boring style of this author to repeat, add a little prose and repeat the main points of his arguments in this book. If you already get it, please forgive your humble author as we may again tell you why you get it.

And, so, post facto, we offer another rationale for the Bill of Rights. For the patient, I suspect each time such a notion is read, substantial learning occurs.

The *Bill of Rights* is what most people think about when they think about the Constitution. In the Bill of Rights, a number of rights are specifically listed though they are already granted implicitly by the Constitution itself. The fundamental rights include *freedom of the press*, *freedom of speech*, *freedom of religion* and other wonderful freedoms that no people on any planet had ever enjoyed until the Founders and Framers christened America.

When the Constitution was ratified on March 4, 1789, it was because several states that held out would not go along until they knew a *bill of rights for US citizens* was coming. Many were concerned that they had given up rights that they already had as written in the Articles of Confederation.

Therefore, the Congress put together twelve amendments to satisfy their needs. Most were worked on by James Madison, who ironically as noted was OK with the bare Constitution with no Bill of Rights. Ten of these bills passed / were ratified and two were rejected. On December 15, 1791, the ten articles in the Bill of Rights were ratified, making these first ten changes part of the US Constitution. Any book about the Constitution must consider all of the debate and the finality of the Bill of Rights.

So, now we say that the first ten constitutional amendments are known collectively as The Bill of Rights. They amplify freedoms for Americans that are and will always be included in the Constitution itself. Yet, in the new millennium America, the way leftist / socialists trample on these lifelines to freedom; one would think they were optional and that the framers cared nothing about them. Yet, this is not the case.

They are not optional. Any amendment becomes part of the overall law of the land, irrevocable by Congress, the President, or the Supreme Court. It is tough to overturn something as unconstitutional when it actually is part of the Constitution.

Despite all the work in assuring freedom for all people, many otherwise intelligent Americans today choose not to understand their hard earned constitutional freedoms. This permits the knaves such as the corrupt politicians in the government, and their backers—the socialist progressive Marxist/communists, enabled by apparent indifference, to handily be taking our rights away. We must stop this encroachment on our liberties.

The *Bill of Rights* may be the key to liberty and freedom, but the Constitution is the lock that shuts government out when it attempts to rule over the people for its own purposes. The Declaration of Independence, The Constitution and The Bill of Rights are intended to make the people supreme and the government subservient.

As we have studied, the US *constitutional system* consists of the power relationships among the principal branches of government resulting from the constitutional division and distribution of political authority among them by the Constitution itself.

It defines the roles in the governing process played by each of the principal governmental institutions defined within the Constitution. Americans must understand this in order to protect their personal freedoms. I hope that is why you chose to read The *Constitution 4 Dummmies!* It is easy to be swayed when your source of news is the popular media, who from recent accounts would like there to be no Constitution and no means of protecting the inalienable rights of all Americans. So, the message from this author is to be careful!

This notion is very important for Americans in that the Constitution provides the following attributes of government on our behalf:

- Divides and distributes the authority of government between the central government over the whole nation and the governments of the member-states of the federal union
- Assigns certain governmental powers to the states, while denying them certain other powers
- Assigns certain powers to the national government and expressly prohibits it from exercising *any powers not*

explicitly granted. ----- In other words, the Federal
government cannot by law decide that you cannot use
anything. For example, they have unlawfully decreed
you cannot use incandescent light bulbs as those
invented by Thomas Edison. When the government is
permitted to do things like this that violate personal
freedom, it is operating outside of its constitutional
authority. Since Congress has permitted this and
similar erosions of the people's power, some of US,
and more very day, suggest we call all of our
congressional representatives home and replace them
with a set of people who are not afraid to represent the
real interests of the people.

- Assigns the powers delegated to the national
government to the principal entities of that government
(The U.S. House of Representatives, the U.S. Senate,
the President of the U.S.A., and the U.S. Courts
system, with supreme judicial power reserved for the
Supreme Court). Each entity has its own power, a
strong incentive, and a legal right to oppose, block,
check, and restrain the other entities of government
when they get off track.

- Prescribes certain limitations on both the central
government and the states by guaranteeing *civil liberties*,
i.e., the basic rights and liberties of the individual
citizen.

Facets of the constitutionality of the government may be
overridden in fact if not in deed. The current President has
chosen to ignore Congress and not to follow the Constitution
as the implicit enforcer of law in America.

The Congress, choosing to be an inept body for several years
prior to and including 2014, enabled the President's power
grab through inaction—though it remains unconstitutional.

Power abuse will continue until the people (US) vote out all
members of the assembly who are in line with the ideology of

a lawless president. The US government must comply with
two fundamental legal requirements to remain legitimate

— The government must operate in accordance with
the provisions of the Constitution
— The government must not exceed the authority
granted to it by the Constitution.

The bottom line unfortunately for all Americans is that our
government can be declared illegitimate since it complies with
neither of these requirements. Check the news sources. Check
the blogs. Check the White House logs. This Administration
points its middle finger at the Constitution and that makes it
illegitimate. See the two provisions above.

As much as we may personally like our representatives, we do
not want them taking more power than we are willing to give
them. When you read the Constitution, it is clear how
insightful the Founding Fathers were as they built the
essential features of constitutionalism into the framework of
the US government. The government's compliance with these
two basic legal requirements is essential to its legitimacy.

Government can do as it may choose if unchecked. The
people must check mate the government by sending reputable,
non-politicians to represent US.

So if we were to summarize the central purpose of
constitutionalism in 2014 / 2015 , it would begin by sounding
like this.

> *It is to protect ourselves from our too-far-
> reaching neighbors who become politicians to
> promote their own welfare.*

The notion of limiting governmental power as dictated in the
Constitution checks and restrains the persons who hold public
office and who exercise political authority.

Thus, it is up to all of US as a wary and watchful society that our otherwise wonderful government does not get out of control. Hopefully, this book will help US all in this regard. America is not supposed to be a place for dummmies. It is a place where all people are given the opportunity to be the best and the brightest. Our Constitution provides for this.

The Constitution of our wonderful union of states has protected us for so long (well over 200 years) that we take it for granted. Progressive, aka communist leaders on the left, hoping we are all dummmies are hoping to rob US of our inalienable rights so they can add to their wallets, and their personal opportunities. If they cared as much about We the People, America would be a far better place in which to live.

The first constitutional battle

If you think you heard this already, you are right. But, like all good stories, the more times you hear it, the more believable it becomes. This again is the constitutional battle of those for a Bill of Rights and those against it. It is a battle worth rehearing.

As we continue to summarize the battle for the Bill of Rights, just a few years after the Constitution was written and approved by the convention, a new political battle had ensued. It pitted the Founding Fathers against one another and threatened the ratification of the document over which they'd wrestled so hard and long to create.

The Federalists, including James Madison, George Washington and Alexander Hamilton, feared that if some rights were listed, others not explicitly enumerated would be left vulnerable. On the other side, the Anti-federalists, including George Mason, Thomas Jefferson and Patrick Henry, were adamant that the Constitution must explicitly guarantee certain fundamental rights that no government could take away. They believed that not listing rights risked there being no rights.

Out of it all, ten of the twelve notions brought forward to the Congress were approved and later ratified by the states. The Bill of Rights is a hallmark of our Democratic Republic, and never were so many Constitutional Amendments approved by the Congress and ratified by the states in such short order

In the end, we have the US Constitution!

At the end of the Constitutional Convention in 1789, Benjamin Franklin, a great Founder from Pennsylvania, wrote:

"It is a singular thing in the history of mankind that a great people have had the opportunity of forming a government for themselves. We are making experiment in politics. In these sentiments, I agree to this Constitution, with all its faults, if they are such. For when you assemble a number of men to have the advantage of their joint wisdom, you inevitably assemble with those men all their prejudices, their passions, their errors of opinion, their local interests, and their selfish views. It therefore astonishes me to find this system approaching so near to perfection as it does."

Franklin also warned, "We must all hang together, or most assuredly we shall all hang separately."

Chapter 15

Summary of All 27 Amendments to the Constitution

Can such great works be summarized?

Without reading the full text of an amendment, one cannot gain its full impact on the freedoms and rights of American citizens. Even then, for average Joe's, such verbiage is tough to read.

Though the amendments to the Constitution can be summarized, it is for purposes other than understanding their full impact on the nation. It is for a perspective on what they contain from cover to cover without having to read all between. Like all summaries, citizens get to read about the nature and the planned purposes of the amendments even without reading them. So, summaries do have value.

The summaries do not give the notion of the full text of the principles of our government for sure but they show where correction was needed and applied. The Founders admitted that they were imperfect. All humans are imperfect. So, when the founders created the Articles of Confederation to govern the United States, it was round one of an effort to make a more perfect democratic republic.

As humans, after a time, even the Founders doubted the perfection of their resulting work. Nobody delivers perfection, ever, only God. So, should the founders have given up and said c'est la vie (French for that's just how it is)—when the Articles of Confederation were deemed imperfect? Should they have gone home, opened up a bottle of the finest wine and approved of themselves to the bottom of the bottle. Or should have taken another try to do better? Of course, we all vote for the latter and so did the Founders.

There is nothing like the original and that is why in preceding chapters we discuss the Constitution as written, prior to the Bill of Rights. The Bill of Rights certainly has helped the hoi polloi and the hoity-toity understand this major historical document far better.

In the appendices of this book, there is much text which further explains the position of the Bill of Rights in context with the US Constitution. The Constitution improved on the Articles of Confederation, and the Bill of Rights clarified for the common man, the implicit rights inherent in the Constitution.

The Bill of Rights has been fully explained in their purpose and their meaning in this and preceding chapters of this book. It is a feel good document for scholars but it is an essential document for Americans searching for just a few well written sentences describing their rights.

The Bill of Rights changed the Constitution to make it clear that Americans had specific rights, not just those denied to the federal government through the Constitution. The US government, over the next two hundred plus years from the Constitution's ratification found just seventeen additional changes to the Constitution necessary once the Bill of Rights became the first ten amendments.

These of course were in addition to the ten amendments (changes) already included in the Bill of Rights. These twenty-seven amendments make the US Constitution an even better, and an even more perfect union of the United States of

America than the Constitution itself, when it replaced the
Articles of Confederation.

Let's take a quick snapshot of the entire twenty-seven
Amendments including the first ten, the Bill of Rights.
Besides the Constitution itself, these are the outward
principles upon which our freedoms and our liberties are cast.

The Bill of Rights in summary:

Amendment I: Freedom of speech, religion, press, petition,
assembly.
Amendment II: Right to bear arms and militia.
Amendment III: Quartering of soldiers.
Amendment IV: Warrants and searches.
Amendment V: Individual debt and double jeopardy.
Amendment VI: Speedy trial, witnesses and accusations.
Amendment VII: Right for a jury trial.
Amendment VIII: Bail and fines.
Amendment IX: Existence of other rights for the people
Amendment X: Power reserved to the states and people.

Later amendments in summary

Amendment XI: Suits against states.
Amendment XII: Election of executive branch.
Amendment XIII: Prohibition of slavery.
Amendment XIV: Privileges or immunities, due process,
elections and debt: Consists of 5 sections and defines: (1)
Citizenship (2) Apportionment of representatives among
the states, (3) Rules for being a senator or representative,
(4) Validity of the public debt, (5) Congressional
enforcement of this Article.

Amendment XV: Race and the right to vote.
Amendment XVI: US Income tax enabled.
Amendment XVII: Senator election change and number.
Amendment XVIII: Prohibition on sale of alcohol
Amendment XIX: Gender and the right to vote.
Amendment XX: "Lame duck" Congress eliminated.
Amendment XXI: Repeal of Amendment XVIII (Prohibition).
Amendment XXII: Limit of Presidential terms.
Amendment XXIII: Election rules for the District of Columbia
Amendment XXIV: Taxes and the right to vote.
Amendment XXV: Rules of Presidential succession.
Amendment XXVI: Age and the right to vote.
Amendment XXVII: Pay raises and Congress

Amendments Never Ratified

Besides the above summary of the constitutional body of law, six other amendments have been proposed to the Constitution that have not been ratified and thus do not represent the law of the land. The entire text of these amendments is included in Appendix F.

The original first amendment was never ratified. It set the ratio of representatives of Congress to constituents. If this amendment had made it to the bill of Rights, and been ratified, the number of members of the House of Representatives could by now be over 6,000, compared to the present 435. As apportioned by the 2000 Census, each member of the House currently represents about 650,000 people.

The original second amendment passed by Congress which was not ratified, was eventually ratified as the 27th amendment of the United States 203 years after it was first offered. It has to do with Congressional Salaries.

What does all this mean?

We have examined the founding and the revolution and the articles and precepts in the Constitution as the primary law of the land. We have also examined the Bill of rights in detail and the other amendments to the Constitution in summary form.

The Federalist Papers

Most Americans already know that our nation today is in peril; yet many Americans choose not to believe this is the case. For those who see it as it is, *tyranny in our highest federal offices*, it would help for all of US to reread the Declaration of Independence and the Constitution, and the Bill of Rights. We have examined each of these in detail in this book. And so all readers, at this point of this book are already qualified to see the current goings-on, as tyranny pure and simple.

Would the Founders have expected this? To know more about what was on the minds of the Founders when they put forth this great Constitution, and the Bill of Rights, there is only one real way to almost crawl into the pure minds of our Founders.

As you have learned so far, the Founders and the Constitution Framers never expected corruption to interfere with the many checks and balances they had prepared for America and had written into the Constitution and the Bill of Rights. Yet, here we are, a lawless and lying presidential office and tyranny that we have not seen since England was our master.

To know what the founders thought in the 1780's when all of the great ideas were flowing, I would suggest that your next reading ventures be *The Federalist Papers* to help you know the thought process of the Framers when they built the US

Constitution. In this way, you will better understand the Constitution.

My Publisher, Let Go Publish has one of the many books with the entire text of the federalist Papers by Hamilton, Jay, and Madison available to all for reading. www.letsgopublish.com. I edited this book but it is merely the original with some paragraph easing and a lengthy introduction that I wrote.

My book is called *The Federalist Papers by Hamilton, Jay, and Madison.* I admit that I wrote a compelling introduction to the book and edited the many pages of the essays for punctuation. I also shortened one and two page paragraphs into smaller chunks to make them much more readable.

You do not have to buy this book because the Federalist Papers are free on the Internet. If you would like a nice keepsake, however, you can purchase my book at www.bookhawkers,com. To be fair, you can also purchase many other books regarding the Federalist Papers. Some are not quite so easy to read and some are reasonably easy to read. They are sold at many sources on the Internet.

You can also read the entire set of The Federalist Papers online. The following URL is excellent: http://www.constitution.org/fed/federa00.htm Obviously, I would prefer you to read my book, but it is not your only option and in some cases, it is not your least expensive option.

The Constitution was clearly a gift from God. Even Back in 1787, a number of states had sent detailed written plans for the Constitution along with their delegates to the Constitutional Convention in Philadelphia. The Convention began on May 25, 1787 and lasted until September 17, 1787. On September 17, 1787, the state delegates approved the Constitution as written by Madison et al in its final form. The Framers had completed their work and sent the document back to the individual states to be ratified. They then adjourned the convention.

Convincing the Public

The commencing of the Federalist Papers began shortly thereafter. The writing of the papers was commissioned by Alexander Hamilton, a great patriot, who knew he could not write all of the arguments necessary for the people to choose to agree to back the Constitution. Hamilton, and James Madison, and John Jay together wrote **The Federalist Papers** to defend and explain the newly drafted Federal Constitution, and to promote its ratification in the state of New York. A group of folks just as patriotic but against the Constitution were known as the anti-Federalists.

Each of the papers was written as an essay, but when published they became articles in New York newspapers and magazines. Because New York at the time and to this day is a huge and prosperous state, their being published in NY was very important to the ratification of the Constitution. Thus for the writers, it was the major objective of their attention at the time.

The Federalist Papers, written by Alexander Hamilton, John Jay, and James Madison answered the debated questions as posed by the opposition in great detail while copious detractors wrote their own essays / articles in rebuttal. As noted above, and worth repeating, the opposition articles collectively are known as the Anti-Federalist Papers.

Many were published in the press so to offer other thoughts on such an important issue.

Nowhere was the furor over the proposed Constitution in the few states of the US more intense than in New York. Governor George Clinton was very concerned that the state's influence would be compromised at the Constitutional Convention.

The NY Legislature selected State Supreme Court Judge Robert Yates and John Lansing, Speaker of the NY Assembly; to attend the convention. Both were well known Anti-Federalists. Their selection was seen by many as a way for New York to be able to outvote Alexander Hamilton.

There were those, such as Yates and Lansing, whose opposition to the new document was based on their view that the Constitution diminished the rights that Americans had won in the Revolution. The Federalist Papers presented a view that this was not true while the Anti-Federalist Papers, also displayed in popular newspapers of the day, presented a view that the Constitution was bad for America and offered its specific notions.

Alexander Hamilton became fearful that the cause for the Constitution might be lost in his home state of New York. And to be repetitive for learning purposes, this was his purpose in putting together the Federalist Papers.

Hamilton published his first "Federalist" essay in the New York Independent Journal on October 27, 1787

The Federalist, also called *The Federalist Papers*, has served two very different purposes in American history. The 85 essays succeeded in helping to persuade doubtful New Yorkers (as well as the public in the other states), despite the well written efforts of the Anti-Federalists, to ratify the Constitution.

Today, The Federalist Papers help the rest of US to more clearly understand what the writers of the Constitution had in mind when they drafted this amazing document more than 225 years ago.

"America- if we cannot define Liberty, we cannot defend it. If we cannot define tyranny, we cannot defeat it- "KrisAnne Hall www.conservativeactionalerts.com/author/krisanne-hall

"If a nation expects to be ignorant and free, in a state of civilization, it expects what never was and never will be."
- Thomas Jefferson

Let us all be smart. Let us pay attention, and let us continue to be free with unlimited liberty in the finest country that God ever permitted being founded.

Part VI: Lessons & Questions of The Constitution

Chapter 16

Principles of a Constitutional Democracy / Republic

Constitutional Democracy v Democracy

In Chapter 2 we discussed some of the principles of a constitutional representative democracy—aka a Republic. We learned that a democracy is a system of government by the whole population or all the eligible members of a state, typically through elected representatives. In most democracies, majority rule is a major precept and there is little room for a minority viewpoint. The United States is not such a Democracy. The United States is a constitutional representative democracy, which is a *republic*.

Now that we have defined the notion of a democracy, what then makes a constitutional democracy that much different than a "plain democracy?" A constitutional democracy can be described accurately as a system of government in which the power of government is defined and thus _limited_, and it is distributed in a body of fundamental written law called a constitution. In our constitutional representative democracy our body of laws is known as *The Constitution.*

Additionally, the electorate (that's US - the people -- a.k.a. the general voting populace within our political society) is given the effective means of controlling the elected representatives in the government. It also gives US the means to hold them accountable for their decisions and actions while in public office.

A constitutional democracy thus has two essential ingredients, (1) a *constitutional* ingredient and (2) a *democratic* ingredient. Let's examine these two ingredients:

The **constitutional** ingredient of a constitutional democracy is the "*constitutional government*." As noted above, this means that the Founding Fathers wrote a constitution so that the elected representatives of this nation could not just go ahead and do whatever they pleased with complete disregard to the most basic laws of this country—as written in our Constitution. In other words, even a US president would be breaking the law if they took any law, such as Obamacare, or a prisoner exchange, or immigration, and changed the law to suit their own political needs.

The **democratic** ingredient of a constitutional democracy is *representative democracy* and, it has to do with who holds and thus has the right to exercise authority on behalf of the governed. It also describes how such authority is acquired and retained (elections, impeachments etc.). Additionally it prescribes that the representatives of the people are accountable to the people, and through elections, the people can change the face of the government by changing the face of its representatives.

A constitution is a very important document in that it provides the opportunity to protect liberty and freedom beyond the lives of the founders of the government. There is a specific process for constitutional amendments because they are such serious changes in government. That's why to this day, only twenty seven amendments have passed the test of the people.

For the United States of America, its Constitution is the supreme law of land. Thus, it is of higher importance and takes precedence over all other laws of society. In fact, all other laws, to be valid and enforceable, must be written in accordance with the superior law of the Constitution.

Separation of Powers for Honesty

Our Constitution requires a separation of powers, counting on the notion of countervailing power to keep all three separate branches (Executive, Legislative, and Judicial) of government honest. Separation of powers is thus the structure of the government defined by the Constitution with specific powers to each branch, yet with none of the branches having supreme power.

The founders believed for example that the Congress would not let the President act in an unauthorized manner and vice versa. The court was there to solve conflicts within the branches, though it was not given supreme power.

The Legislators in both houses of Congress pass the laws and the president gets an opportunity to veto them or sign them into law. The president gets to hire a staff to enforce the laws. The president does not have the right to construct laws of his own. Only the Congress can pass laws. The Supreme Court (nine members) cannot make laws and cannot enforce them. It can affirm them and it can strike them down if they are deemed unconstitutional.

Within the Congress, the House, with 435 representatives elected by the people based on the population of the states, is the only branch of government permitted to allocate dollars towards funding the laws and the mission of the government.

Thus, the House is in control of the treasury, or the purse as some like to call it. Nothing gets done without money in government, and the House controls the money, and this is so ordained by the Constitution.

The Senate, comprised of 100 Senators, two each from each of the fifty states of the union, is where the voice of the minority is heard. Until recently, 60% of the Senators would have to approve many of the laws / appointments. This is thus not sole majority rule. It gives the minority a voice in the government, as so desired by the founders.

Legislators in the House are elected to two year terms; Senators are elected by the people for six years; and the Supreme Court gets to function for a lifetime after being appointed by the President with the consent of the Senate. Notice the notion of countervailing power.

It is a good notion in government that nobody trusts anybody else because over time, leaders become corrupt. The people today are the ones who have created all of our problems because until it is put right in our faces, we do not believe it is happening. When the people toughen up and pay attention, the scoundrels in government will be check-mated.

Constitutional sniff test needs true nostrils

In a number of relatively recent cases, laws were passed about matters of great importance to all people. These include abortion and marriage gender choice. These have been appealed to the courts and some to the Supreme Court of the U.S. This is right now deemed by practice, not by the Founders intention as the court of last resort.

This court determines whether laws pass the constitutional sniff test. I repeat that the Founders did not intend for the US Supreme Court to be the most powerful branch of government.

However, constitutional scholars believe that the Supreme Court has taken on more power than granted and it has begun to be a partisan to politics. In other words the Supreme Court of the US, aka, SCOTUS, has become grabby and a bit dirty in practice. This had not been the case for most of our 225 + year history. Right now, the court is dirty and embroiled in partisan politics, and nobody at the time of the Founders thought this would ever happen.

As the SCOTUS permits its own political bias to stand in the way of impartial judgment, it is not operating according to the Constitution. Unfortunately, even the Supreme Court understands that as the Supreme Court, the members can lie and the verdicts can be adulterated, but nobody can appeal a verdict to a higher court. And so, our justices have become political and without a lot of guts, regular honest lawyers have a tough time taking them on.

The Founders expected that the justices would be honest and impartial because of their high station in life, and they would always be independent advocates for America. This subtle change, in which ideology has overtaken the freedom and liberty and the power of the people, is of grave concern to the continuance of our constitutional republic.

When the laws do not pass the sniff test or when the political makeup of the court sees things in a different light than the lawmakers, or prior justices, laws created either by the states or by the federal legislature may be affirmed or struck down.

When not upheld, they are no longer in force and thus they cannot be enforced. The President's executive team no longer is compelled to make sure overturned laws are enforced. Many of US in the onlooker category think that the Supreme Court should not take on more power than the Congress since the Congress is the direct voice of the people. When the Supreme Court goes bad, to whom do we appeal? And so we see, though more perfect, the Constitution is not 100% perfect as it relies on the goodness of man to gain perfection.

A proper resolution for the court might be to defer a law at least once, maybe several times, or until the legislature gets it right. In this way, the Congress gets to debate it again and vote on it again. This would solve a lot of problems and would dispel the notion that the Supreme Court is the most powerful branch of a government designed with three equal partners. Of course, just like a presidential veto, if the legislature sends laws back to the court with a major majority, it should no longer be the court's prerogative to rule. That is real separation of power.

Regarding enforcement of the laws, a great example comes from the case of April 16, 2007. The Supreme Court chose to uphold a law that banned a type of late-term abortion, a ruling that many believe portends enormous social, legal and political implications regarding this very divisive issue.

Considering that the nine members of the court itself were sharply divided (5-4) could prove historic. Political analysts suggested at the time that it sent a possible signal of the court's willingness, under Chief Justice John Roberts, to someday revisit the right to abortion which heretofore had been guaranteed in the 1973 Roe v. Wade case.

On Monday, January 31, 2011, U.S. many are aware that district judge Roger Vinson threw out the nation's health care law, known as Obamacare declaring it unconstitutional because it violates the Commerce Clause and surely reviving a feud among competing philosophies about the role of government.

This judge, in Pensacola, Fla., ruled that as a result of the unconstitutionality of the "individual mandate" that requires people to buy insurance, the entire law must be declared void. This did not happen because another case was decided by the SCOTUS. It had been at the appellate level.

In another major case ruling, on June 28, 2012, the Supreme Court upheld Obamacare's individual mandate as a tax. In the case—*The National Federation of Independent Business (NFIB) v. Sebelius* (the official name of the ObamaCare supreme Court Ruling on Obamacare)—the SCOTUS upheld most of the bill. The Supremes rule is final. The final ruling on Obamacare was made by Supreme Court Justice John Roberts who sided with the liberal justices on the court.

The basic idea of the ruling was that Obamacare was declared a tax and not a mandate and was therefore declared constitutional, and citizens were obliged to pay the tax. As you can see, the Supreme Court is very active in matters that many think should be decided by Congress.

Only appealed laws can be declared unconstitutional.

No branch of government is exempt from following the Constitution. In the US, every law enacted by a legislature and every decision or action of an executive office or agency must pass the constitutional test. Not all laws that may be unconstitutional by definition if well examined, however, are challenged in court. The Supreme Court does not go searching for cases. The cases come to the Court.

For a law to be reversed it must be appealed and it can be appealed as many times as needed until it may reach the Supreme Court of the United States. Appeals start at lower courts and progress if accepted by justices at various levels and to the Supreme Court.

If the governmental decision or law or action in question is found by the courts to be contrary to the Constitution, the court system will uphold the Constitution and set aside the unconstitutional verdict or action of the federal or state legislature or of the executive branches.

Unfortunately, as hinted before, many justices of the Supreme Court have decided in recent years to become pawns of government administrations (Clinton, Bush, Obama, etc.), rather than deciding cases for the benefit of the people. After all, these administrations bequeathed upon the appointed justice a wonderful lifelong position.

For example, conservatives never expect that Justice Elena Kagan, the current president's last appointee, will ever vote in a way that Barack Obama's minions have not directed her. Since this is a book of facts, and few opinions, feel free to check this Justice's record.

And so, with Justices of the Supreme Court professing their ideology rather than their adherence to the founding principles, one could logically deduce that the Funders be damned if such ideologues could find enough other ideologues to undermine the country. The above is all fact. And so, we the people must pay attention forever to prevent this from happening. Without our vigilance, politicians are more powerful than they should be.

Back in historical times, American politicians could be considered honest and even honorable because honesty was at the time a virtue. Justices of the Supreme Court were beyond ideology and thus beyond reproach. At least theoretically, they represented the best interests of the people. Today, that unfortunately is not the case. For those learning about America for the first time, we can get back to those days if we choose, but it will not be easy, and it is up to us.

My opinion is that we are at a point in history that the elite in America (not the good elite as in colonial times but the nose in the air, wealthy elite), ruled by those who are not as concerned about America as they are about their own ideologies, have figured out ways to undermine the general population and go against the people.

They use tricks to attract the low information voter segment of "We the People," aka, big dummmies, to their side, and their tactics in appealing to such folks has delivered many elections to them. It is unethical and the Founders, if they could be consulted, would not approve.

Leftists in control of our government are so convinced that people want to stay dummm and continue in this faux love-fest that they are now moving their agendas into the front lines. Somehow they are able to convince the dummmest of Americans to work against the good of the country. Before we can begin to right this, everybody must decide to smarten up and help the low-information segment of our population to be careful what they believe.

It is very important for all Americans to be smart and to refuse to be dummmed down. When the sales pitch is continual, like the millions of advertising dollars spent on Obamacare, logic dictates that it cannot be good for the people. All of the people know their own intelligence levels. If you do not respect your own intelligence, and you want to do right by America, talk to your brother or sister or dad or mom or best friends. Please do not let the communists in this progressive government suck you into something that hurts America.

States Also Have Constitutions

Leftists operating as Americans in America do not like either the Constitution or the Bill of Rights. If the idea of a constitution were so bad, why would it be that each state in our United States of America would have signed up fo the US Constitution and agreed to abide by it. If the idea of constitution were so bad, why would each state have its own constitution?

The answer is obvious of course. It is not a bad idea. It is in fact a great idea! It is the only thing in our great republic that assures us all that our rights come before the rights of corrupt politicians.

Each state in the Union of States has its own constitution thus giving the 50 states (or 57 according to our current president) a notion of semi-autonomy meaning partial self-government. These 50 or 57 states comprise the federal union. Why the President thinks there are 57 states is ample proof to me that we have been doing a bad job in America teaching civics for an awful lot of years. Then again, some might argue that the President received his civics education in another land mass.

The US Constitution guides the operation of the national government, and establishes its formal power relationships between the three branches of the national government as well as among the 50 semiautonomous states as well as the formal power relationships among the other principal organs, or institutions, of the national government. None of US would want this left to folklore or to memory alone as it is far too important. Thus it is written—and yes, it is law! And once a law is written, it must be enforced by a willing president, or the system does not work.

The U.S. Constitution is in fact, a single document consisting of the seven original articles drafted by the Federal Constitutional Convention of 1787, which were eventually ratified by the 13 original colonies (states), plus there are 27 amendments that have been added to the document during the 225 + years that have elapsed since original ratification and adoption of the Constitution.

Chapter 17

Q & A on The Constitution, The Bill Of Rights & More!   Part I of II

Questions & Answers Pertaining to the Constitution

by Sol Bloom

Sol Bloom was a US Congressman from NY's 19th District for twenty seven years until his death in 1949. He presided over the US Constitution's Sesquicentennial Exposition (1937 – one-hundred-and-fiftieth anniversary), serving as its Chairman. He is well known for being the author of *The Story of the Constitution.* For those of you looking for more reading about this great document, please note that Mr. Bloom's work is well respected.

His popular history book was first published in 1937 in honor of the 150th anniversary of the creation of the U.S. Constitution. "It is a book for the people," wrote Bloom to describe his work. "Accordingly, it tells briefly the origins of our country and what the steps were that led up to the formation of the Constitution. Having told how and why the national government came about, the book tells what the Constitution stands for, its principles, and the means by which it operates."

The original book was a classic in constitutional studies. It is 6" x 9", 192 pages, with 51 illustrations. It was reprinted by the National Archives and Records Administration in

1986. It is in the public domain, and so it can be read and copied for free. My plan is to transcribe the book and make it available on www.bookhawkers.com sometime in the next year.

In one of the first Q & A's, such as those we would find on the Internet today, Sol Bloom published his "Questions & Answers Pertaining to the Constitution." These are very good questions and Bloom's answers are right on the money. Since this work is public domain and since the questions are those that many readers of this book would find interesting, I have included all Bloom's questions and answers below. Enjoy:

Bloom's Constitutional Q&A

Q. How were deputies to the Constitutional Convention chosen?
A. They were appointed by the legislatures of the different States.

Q. Were there any restrictions as to the number of deputies a State might send?
A. No.

Q. Which State did not send deputies to the Constitutional Convention?
A. Rhode Island and Providence Plantations.

Q. Were the other twelve States represented throughout the Constitutional Convention?
A. No. Two of the deputies from New York left on July 10, 1787, and after that Hamilton, the third deputy, when he was in attendance did not attempt to cast the vote of his State. The New Hampshire deputies did not arrive until July 23, 1787; so that there never was a vote of more than eleven States.

Q. Where and when did the deputies to the Constitutional Convention assemble?
A. In Philadelphia, in the State House where the Declaration of Independence was signed. The meeting was called for May 14, 1787, but a quorum was not present until May 25.

Q. About how large was the population of Philadelphia?
A. The census of 1790 gave it 28,000; including its suburbs, about 42,000.

Q. What was the average age of the deputies to the Constitutional Convention?
A. About 44.

Q. Who were the oldest and youngest members of the Constitutional Convention?
A. Benjamin Franklin, of Pennsylvania, then 81; and Jonathan Dayton, of New Jersey, 26.

Q. How many lawyers were members of the Constitutional Convention?
A. There were probably 34, out of 55, who had at least made a study of the law.

Q. From what classes of society were the members of the Constitutional Convention drawn?
A. In addition to the lawyers, there were soldiers, planters, educators, ministers, physicians, financiers, and merchants.

Q. How many members of the Constitutional Convention had been members of the Continental Congress?
A. Forty, and two others were later members.

Q. Were there any members of the Constitutional Convention who never attended any of its meetings?
A. There were nineteen who were never present. Some of these declined, others merely neglected the duty.

Q. Were the members of the Constitutional Convention called "delegates" or "deputies," and is there any distinction between the terms?
A. Some of the States called their representatives "delegates"; some, "deputies"; and some, "commissioners," the terms being often mixed. In the Convention itself they were always referred to as "deputies." Washington, for example, signed his name as "deputy from Virginia." The point is simply that whatever they called themselves, they were representatives of their States. The general practice of historians is to describe them as "delegates."

Q. Who was called the "Sage of the Constitutional Convention"?
A. Benjamin Franklin, of Pennsylvania.

Q. Who was called the "Father of the Constitution"?
A. James Madison, of Virginia, because in point of erudition and actual contributions to the formation of the Constitution he was preeminent.

Q. Was Thomas Jefferson a member of the Constitutional Convention?
A. No. Jefferson was American Minister to France at the time of the Constitutional Convention.

Q. What did Thomas Jefferson have to do with framing the Constitution?
A. Although absent from the Constitutional Convention and during the period of ratification, Jefferson rendered no inconsiderable service to the cause of Constitutional Government, for it was partly through his insistence that the Bill of Rights, consisting of the first ten amendments, was adopted.

Q. Who presided over the Constitutional Convention?
A. George Washington, chosen unanimously.

Q. How long did it take to frame the Constitution?
A. It was drafted in fewer than one hundred working days.

Q. How much was paid for the journal kept by Madison during the Constitutional Convention?
A. President Jackson secured from Congress in 1837 an appropriation of $30,000 with which to buy Madison's journal and other papers left by him.

Q. Was there harmony in the Convention?
A. Serious conflicts arose at the outset, especially between those representing the small and large States.

Q. Who presented the Virginia Plan?
A. Edmund Randolph.

Q. What was the Connecticut Compromise?
A. This was the first great compromise of the Constitutional Convention, whereby it was agreed that in the Senate each State should have two members, and that in the House the number of Representatives was to be based upon population. Thus the rights of the small States were safeguarded, and the majority of the population was to be fairly represented.

Q. Who actually wrote the Constitution?
A. In none of the relatively meager records of the Constitutional Convention is the literary authorship of any part of the Constitution definitely established. The deputies debated proposed plans until, on July 24, 1787, substantial agreement having been reached, a Committee of Detail was appointed, consisting of John Rutledge, of South Carolina; Edmund Randolph, of Virginia; Nathaniel Gorham, of Massachusetts; Oliver Ellsworth, of Connecticut; and James Wilson, of Pennsylvania, who on August 6 reported a draft which included a Preamble and twenty-three articles, embodying fifty-seven sections. Debate continued until September 8, when a new Committee of Style was named to revise the draft. This committee included William Samuel Johnson, of Connecticut; Alexander Hamilton, of New York; Governor Morris, of Pennsylvania; James Madison, of Virginia; and Rufus King, of Massachusetts, and they reported the draft in approximately its final shape on September 12. The actual literary form is believed to be largely that of Morris, and the chief testimony for this is in the letters

and papers of Madison, and Morris's claim. However, the document in reality was built slowly and laboriously, with not a piece of material included until it has been shaped and approved. The preamble was written by the Committee of Style.

Q. Who was the penman who, after the text of the Constitution had been agreed on, engrossed it prior to the signing?
A. Jacob Shallus who, at the time, was assistant clerk of the Pennsylvania State Assembly, and whose office was in the same building in which the Convention was held.

Q. Does his name appear on the document or in any of the papers pertaining to its preparation?
A. No. In the financial memoranda there is an entry of $30 for "clerks employed to transcribe & engross."

Q. When and how was the identity of the engrosser determined?
A. In 1937, on the occasion of the 150th anniversary of the Constitution. His identity was determined after a long and careful search of collateral public documents, and is here disclosed for the first time.

Q. Where did Shallus do the engrossing?
A. There is no record of this, but probably in Independence Hall.

Q. Did he realize the importance of the work he had done?
A. Probably not; when he died, in 1796, the Constitution had not yet come to be the firmly established set of governmental principles it since has become.

Q. Did some of the deputies to the Constitutional Convention refuse to sign the Constitution?
A. Only thirty-nine signed. Fourteen deputies had departed for their homes, and three--Randolph and Mason, of Virginia, and Gerry, of Massachusetts--refused to sign. One of the signatures is that of an absent deputy, John Dickinson, of Delaware, added at his request by George Read, who also was from Delaware.

Q. How can it be said that the signing of the Constitution was unanimous, when the deputies of only twelve States signed and some delegates refused to sign?
A. The signatures attest the "Unanimous Consent of the States present." The voting was by States, and the vote of each State that of a majority of its deputies. Hamilton signed this attestation for New York, though as he was the only deputy of the State present he had not been able to cast the vote of his State for the consent, only eleven States voting on the final question. There is an even greater discrepancy about the Signers of the Declaration of Independence. Some seven or eight members present on July 4 never signed; seven Signers, including Richard Henry Lee, of Virginia, who proposed the resolution

of independence, were not present on the day; and eight other Signers were not members of Congress until after July 4.

Q. Did George Washington sign the Declaration of Independence?
A. No. He had been appointed Commander-in-Chief of the Continental Army more than a year before and was at the time with the army in New York City.

Q. What are the exact measurements of the originals of the Declaration of Independence and of the Constitution of the United States?
A. The Declaration of Independence: 29 7/8 in. by 24 7/16 in.; The Constitution: four sheets, approximately 28 3/4 in. by 23 5/8 in. each.

Q. How many words are there in the texts in the present volume, and how long does it take to read them?
A. The Constitution has 4,543 words, including the signatures but not the certificate on the interlineations; and takes about half an hour to read. The Declaration of Independence has 1,458 words, with the signatures, but is slower reading, as it takes about ten minutes. The Farewell Address has 7,641 words and requires forty-five minutes to read.

Q. What party names were given to those who favored ratification and to those who opposed it?
A. Those who favored ratification were called Federalists; those who opposed, Anti-federalists.

Q. In ratifying the Constitution, did the people vote directly?
A. No. Ratification was by special State conventions (Art. VII).

Q. The vote of how many States was necessary to ratify the Constitution?
A. Nine (Art. VII).

Q. In what order did the States ratify the Constitution?
A. In the following order: Delaware, Pennsylvania, New Jersey, Georgia, Connecticut, Massachusetts, Maryland, South Carolina, New Hampshire, Virginia, and New York. After Washington had been inaugurated, North Carolina and Rhode Island ratified.

Q. After the Constitution was submitted for ratification, where did the greatest contests occur?
A. In Massachusetts, Virginia, and New York.

Q. In each instance what was the vote?
A. New York ratified the Constitution by a majority of three votes 30 to 27; Massachusetts by 187 to 168; and Virginia by 89 to 79.

Q. In the course of ratification, how many amendments were offered by the State conventions?
A. Seventy-eight; exclusive of Rhode Island's twenty-one, and those demanded by the first convention in North Carolina. There were many others offered which were considered necessary as items of a Bill of

Rights. Professor Ames gives 124 as the whole number, inclusive of those of Rhode Island and North Carolina and the Bills of Rights. Various of these covered the same topics.

Q. When did the United States government go into operation under the Constitution?
A. The Constitution became binding upon nine States by the ratification of the ninth State, New Hampshire, June 21, 1788. Notice of this ratification was received by Congress on July 2, 1788. On September 13, 1788, Congress adopted a resolution declaring that electors should be appointed in the ratifying States on the first Wednesday in January, 1789; that the electors vote for President on the first Wednesday in February, 1789; and that "the first Wednesday in March next [March 4, 1789] be the time and the present seat of Congress the place for commencing proceedings under the said constitution."

The Convention had also suggested "that after such Publication the Electors should be appointed, and the Senators and Representatives elected." The Constitution left with the States the control over the election of congressmen, and Congress said nothing about this in its resolution; but the States proceeded to provide for it as well as for the appointment of electors. On March 3, 1789, the old Confederation went out of existence and on March 4 the new government of the United States began legally to function, according to a decision of the Supreme Court of the United States (wings v. Speed, 5 Wheat. 420); however, it had no practical existence until April 6, when first the presence of quorums in both Houses permitted organization of Congress.

On April 30, 1789, George Washington was inaugurated as President of the United States, so on that date the executive branch of the government under the Constitution became operative. But it was not until February 2, 1790, that the Supreme Court, as head of the third branch of the government, organized and, held its first session; so that is the date when our government under the Constitution became fully operative.

Q. Did Washington receive the unanimous vote of the electors in his first election as President?
A. Yes, of all who voted. Four, two in Virginia and two in Maryland, did not vote; and the eight votes to which New York was entitled were not cast because the legislature could come to no agreement upon how the electors should be appointed. There should have been 81 votes; he received 69.

Q. How did the first inauguration proceed?
A. The Senate Journal narrates it as follows: "The House of Representatives, preceded by their Speaker, came into the Senate Chamber, and took the seats assigned them; and the joint Committee, preceded by their Chairman, agreeably to order, introduced the President of the United States to the Senate Chamber, where he was

received by the Vice President, who conducted him to the Chair; when the Vice President informed him, that 'The Senate and House of Representatives were ready to attend him to take the oath required by the Constitution, and that it would be administered by the Chancellor of the State of New-York'--To which the President replied, he was ready to proceed:--and being attended to the gallery in front of the Senate Chamber, by the Vice President and Senators, the Speaker and Representatives, and the other public characters present, the oath was administered.--After which the Chancellor proclaimed, 'Long live George Washington, President of the United States.' The President having returned to his seat, after a short pause, arose and addressed the Senate and House of Representatives . . . The President, the Vice President, the Senate and House of Representatives, &c. then proceeded to St. Paul's Chapel, where divine service was performed by the Chaplain of Congress, after which the President was conducted to his house, by the Committee appointed for that purpose."

Q. Was Adams sworn in as Vice President before Washington took the oath of office as President?
A. No. Neither the Vice President nor any Senators took the oath of office until June 3. The first act of Congress, June 1, provided for the oath. In the House the Speaker and members present on April 8 had taken an oath provided for by a resolve on April 6 of that House, and the act of June 1 recognized that oath as sufficient for those who had taken it.

Q. What cities have been capitals of the United States government?
A. The Continental Congress sat at Philadelphia, 1774-76, 1777, 1778-83; Baltimore, 1776-77; Lancaster, 1777; York, 1777-78; Princeton, 1783; Annapolis, 1783-84; Trenton, 1784; and New York, 1785-89. The first capital under the Constitution of the United States was in New York, but in 1790 it was moved to Philadelphia. Here it was continued until 1800, when the permanent capital, Washington, in the new District of Columbia, was occupied.

Q. How was the manner of address of the President of the United States decided?
A. Both Houses of Congress appointed committees to consider the proper title to give the President, but they could not agree. The Senate wished it to be "His Highness the President of the United States of America and Protector of their Liberties." The House considered this as too monarchical, and on May 5 addressed its reply to the inaugural speech merely to "The President of the United States." The Senate on May 14 agreed to this simple form.

Q. What is meant by the term "constitution"?
A. A constitution embodies the fundamental principles of a government. Our constitution, adopted by the sovereign power, is amendable by that power only. To the constitution all laws, executive actions, and, judicial decisions must conform, as it is the creator of the powers exercised by the departments of government.

Q. Why has our Constitution been classed as "rigid"?
A. The term "rigid" is used in opposition to "flexible" because the provisions are in a written document which cannot be legally changed with the same ease and in the same manner as ordinary laws. The British Constitution, which is unwritten, can, on the other hand, be changed overnight by act of Parliament.

Q. What was W. E. Gladstone's famous remark about the Constitution?
A. It was as follows: "As the British Constitution is the most subtle organism which has proceeded from the womb and long gestation of progressive history, so the American Constitution is, so far as I can see, the most wonderful work ever struck off at a given time by the brain and purpose of man."

Q. What is the source of the philosophy found in the Constitution?
A. The book which had the greatest influence upon the members of the Constitutional Convention was Montesquieu's Spirit of Laws, which first appeared in 1748. The great French philosopher had, however, in turn borrowed much of his doctrine from the Englishman John Locke, with whose writings various members of the Convention were also familiar.

Q. Are there original ideas of government in the Constitution?
A. Yes; but its main origins lie in centuries of experience in government, the lessons of which were brought over from England and further developed through the practices of over a century and a half in the colonies and early State governments, and in the struggles of the Continental Congress. Its roots are deep in the past; and its endurance and the obedience and respect it has won are mainly the result of the slow growth of its principles from before the days of Magna Carta.

Q. In what language was Magna Carta written, and to whom was it addressed?
A. It was written in Latin and was addressed "To the archbishops, bishops, abbots, earls, barons, justices, foresters, sheriffs, reeves, ministers, and to all bailiffs, and faithful subjects."

Q. What part of the world was first called America?
A. The name "America" was first applied to Central Brazil, in honor of Amerigo Vespucci, who claimed its discovery. It was first applied to the whole known western world by Mercator, the geographer, in 1538.

Q. When did the phrase, "The United States of America," originate?
A. The first known use of the formal term "United States of America" was in the Declaration of Independence. Thomas Paine, in February, 1776, had written of "Free and independent States of America." The terms "United Colonies," "United Colonies of America," "United Colonies of North America," and also "States," were used in 1775 and 1776.

Q. What state papers should be considered in connecting the Constitution of the United States with Magna Carta?

A. The Great Charter was confirmed several times by later medieval monarchs, and there were various statutes, such as those of Westminster, which also helped to develop the germs of popular government. The Petition of Right, 1628, against the abuse of the royal prerogative, the Habeas Corpus Act, 1679, and the Bill of Rights, 1689, to establish the claims of the Petition, are the great English documents of more modern times on popular freedom. Meanwhile, the colonial charters became the foundation of the Americans' claim to the "rights of Englishmen," and were the predecessors of the State Constitutions, which owed their origin to the American Revolution. The Declaration of Independence established the principles which the Constitution made practical. Plans for colonial union were proposed from time to time, the most important of them being the Albany Plan of 1754, of which Benjamin Franklin was the author. The united efforts to establish independence gave birth to the Articles of Confederation, which though inadequate, were a real step toward the "more perfect Union" of the Constitution.

Q. In what respect had the Confederation failed?
A. It had three great weaknesses. It had no means of revenue independent of that received through its requisitions on the States, which were nothing more than requests, which the States could and did disregard; and it had no control over foreign or interstate commerce. Behind these lacks was its inability to compel the States to honor the national obligations. It could make treaties but had no means to compel obedience to them; or to provide for the payment of the foreign debt. It had responsibility but no power as a national government; no means of coercing the States to obedience even to the very inadequate grant given to the "League of Friendship" by the Articles of Confederation. But its greatest weakness was that it had no direct origin in, or action on, the people themselves; but, unlike both the Declaration of Independence and the later Constitution, knew only the States and was known only to them, calling them sovereign.

Q. How extensively has the Constitution been copied?
A. All later Constitutions show its influence; it has been copied extensively throughout the world.

Q. The United States government is frequently described as one of limited powers. Is this true?
A. Yes. The United States government possesses only such powers as are specifically granted to it by the Constitution.

Q. Then how does it happen that the government constantly exercises powers not mentioned by the Constitution?
A. Those powers simply flow from general provisions. To take a simple example, the Constitution gives to the United States the right to coin money. It would certainly follow, therefore, that the government had the right to make the design for the coinage. This is what the Supreme Court calls "reasonable construction" of the Constitution (Art. I, sec. 8, cl. 18).

Q. Where, in the Constitution, is there mention of education?
A. There is none; education is a matter reserved for the States.

Q. Who was called the "Expounder of the Constitution"?
A. Daniel Webster, of Massachusetts, because of his forceful and eloquent orations interpreting the document.

Q. Must a member of the House of Representatives be a resident of the district which he represents?
A. The Constitution provides only that no person shall be a representative "who shall not, when elected, be an Inhabitant of that State in which he shall be chosen"; but makes no requirement as to residence within the district (Art. I, sec. 2, cl. 2).

Q. Is it possible to impeach a justice of the Supreme Court?
A. It is possible to impeach a Justice of the Supreme Court or any other official. The Constitution makes provision for impeachment by the House and trial of the accused by the Senate sitting as a court of "all civil Officers," which includes the Justices (Art. I, sec. 2, cl. 5; sec. 3, cl. 6, 7; Art. II, sec. 4).

Q. Are Senators, Representatives, and justices of the Supreme Court civil officials of the United. States?
A. Justices are, but the others are probably not. The Constitution in several places seems to make a clear distinction between legislators and officials, though this has been contested. Members of Congress are not subject to impeachment, but are liable to expulsion by the vote of the House of which they are members (Art. I, sec. 5, cl. 2).

Q. What would be the proceeding in case of the impeachment of a Cabinet officer?
A. An impeachment proceeding may be set in motion in the House of Representatives by charges made on the floor on the responsibility of a member or territorial delegate; by charges preferred by a memorial, which is usually referred to a committee for examination; by charges transmitted by the legislature of a State or from a grand jury; or the facts developed and reported by an investigating committee of the House. After the impeachment has been voted by the House, the case is heard by the Senate sitting as a court. When the President of the United States is impeached and tried, the proceedings are the same except that the Senate is then presided over by the Chief Justice of the United States (Art. I, sec. 2, cl. 5; sec. 3, cl. 6, 7; Art. II, sec. 4).

Q. What is meant when it is said that Senators are paired?
A. Sometimes a Senator belonging to one party agrees with a Senator belonging to the other party that neither will vote if the other is absent, the theory being that they would always vote on opposite sides of the question. This is called a pair. Sometimes pairs are secured on a particular vote only. For example, if a Senator is in favor of a certain piece of legislation and is ill or unavoidably detained, his friends

arrange for some one on the opposite side not to vote. This insures for each a record as to his views. While many are opposed to general pairs, as the first is called, all are glad to arrange a pair for a specific measure if a Senator is unavoidably prevented from being present (Art. I, sec. 5, cl. 2).

Chapter 17

Q & A on The Constitution, The Bill Of Rights & More!   Part II of II

Questions & Answers Pertaining to the Constitution

by Sol Bloom

Q. What is the mace of the House of Representatives and what purpose does it serve?
A. The mace consists of thirteen ebony rods, about three feet long, representing the thirteen original States. It is bound together with silver in imitation of the thongs which bound the fasces of ancient Rome. The shaft is surmounted by a globe of solid silver about five inches in diameter upon which rests a massive silver eagle. The mace is the symbol of the paramount authority of the House within its own sphere. In times of riot or disorder upon the floor the Speaker may direct the Sergeant-at-Arms, the executive officer of the House, to bear the mace up and down the aisles as a reminder that the dignity and decorum of the House must not be overthrown. Defiance to such warning is the ultimate disrespect to the House and may lead to expulsion. When the House is sitting as a body the mace rests upright on a pedestal at the right of the Speaker's dais; when the House is sitting in committee of the whole, the mace stands upon the floor at the foot of its pedestal. Thus, when the House wishes to "rise" from committee of the whole and resume business as a legislative body, lifting the mace to its pedestal automatically effects the transition. The origin of the idea of the mace is based upon a similar emblem in the British House of Commons (Art. I, sec. 5, cl. 2).

Q. Who administers the oath of office to the Speaker of the House of Representatives?
A. It is usually administered by the oldest member in point of service (Art. I, sec. 5, cl. 2).

Q. What is meant by the "Father" of the House of Representatives?
A. It is a colloquial title informally bestowed upon the oldest member in point of service (Art. I, sec. 5, cl. 2). It was borrowed originally from the House of Commons.

Q. Why is a member of the House of Representatives referred to on the floor as "the gentleman from New York," for example, instead of by name?
A. It is a custom in all large deliberative bodies to avoid the use of the personal name in debate or procedure. The original purpose of this was to avoid any possible breach of decorum and to separate the political from the personal character of each member (Art. I, sec. 6, cl. 1).

Q. Do members of Congress get extra compensation for their work on committees?
A. No. (Art. I, sec. 6, cl. 1).

Q. Could members of the President's Cabinet be permitted to sit in Congress without amending the Constitution?
A. No. A national officeholder cannot at the same time be a member of either House of Congress (Art. 1, sec. 6, cl. 2).

Q. Must all revenue and appropriation bills originate in the House of Representatives?
A. The Constitution provides that all bills for raising revenue shall originate in the House of Representatives. It is customary for appropriation bills to originate there also (Art. I, sec. 7, cl. 1).

Q. What is meant by the word veto, in the President's powers?
A. The word is from the Latin and means "I forbid." The President is authorized by the Constitution to refuse his assent to a bill presented by Congress if for any reason he disapproves of it. Congress may, however, pass the act over his veto but it must be by a two-thirds majority in both houses. If Congress adjourns before the end of the 10 days, the President can prevent the enactment of the bill by merely not signing it. This is called a pocket veto. (Art. I, sec. 7, cl. 2).

Q. If, after a bill has passed both houses of Congress and gone to the President, Congress desires to recall it, can this be done?
A. A bill which has reached the President may be recalled only by concurrent resolution. The form used is as follows: Resolved, by the House of Representatives (the Senate concurring), That the President be requested to return to the House of Representatives the bill . . . (title). After the concurrent resolution passes both houses it is formally transmitted to the President. The latter might, however, have already signed it, in which case it would have become a law and would have to be repealed in regular fashion (Art. I, sec. 7, cl. 2).

Q. What is the difference between a joint and a concurrent resolution of Congress?
A. A joint resolution has the same force as an act, and must be signed by the President or passed over his veto. A concurrent resolution is not a law, but only a measure on which the two Houses unite for a purpose

concerned with their organization and procedure, or expressions of facts, principles, opinions, and purposes, "matters peculiarly within the province of Congress alone," and not embracing "legislative provisions proper" (Art. 1, sec. 7, cl. 3).

Q. Which is the longest term of office in the government, aside from judges?
A. The Comptroller General of the United States and the Assistant Comptroller General have the longest tenure. They hold office for fifteen years (Art. I, sec. 8), cl. 18; sec. 9, cl. 7; Art. II, sec. 2, cl. 2).

Q. What is the term of office of Treasurer of the United States?
A. The Treasurer is appointed by the President of the United States, and no length of term of office is specified (Art. I, sec. 8, cl. 18; sec. 9, cl. 7; Art. II, sec. 2, cl. 2).

Q. Does the Constitution provide for the formation of a Cabinet?
A. No. The Constitution vests the executive power in the President. Executive departments were created by successive acts of Congress under authority conferred by the Constitution in Art. I, sec. 8, cl. 18. The Departments of State, Treasury, and War were created by the first session of the First Congress. The Secretaries of these, together with the Attorney General, formed the first President's Cabinet. The Cabinet, it should be distinctly understood, is merely an advisory body whose members hold office only during the pleasure of the President. It has no constitutional function as a Cabinet, and the word does not appear in an act of Congress until February 26, 1907 (Art. I, sec. 8, cl. 18; Art. II, sec. 1, cl. 1, sec. 2, cl. 1).

Q. How many methods of electing the President of the United States were considered by the Constitutional Convention?
A. Five. These were by the Congress; by the people; by State legislatures; by State executives; and by electors. Various methods of appointing the electors were proposed: by popular vote, by lottery from members of Congress, by State legislatures, and by State executives; and the matter was finally compromised by leaving the method to each State legislature. The meeting of the electors in one body was also proposed; and at first the final choice, in case election by electors failed, was given to the Senate, but later, after choice by Congress had been defeated, it was transferred to the House, voting by States.

Q. Who appoints the Chief Justice of the United States and for how long a term?
A. The Chief Justice of the United States and the Associate Justices are appointed for life (during good behavior) by the President of the United States, "by and with the Advice and Consent of the Senate," (Art. II, sec. 2, cl. 2; Art. III, sec. 1).

Q. By what authority may the President of the United States call an extra session of Congress?

A. The Constitution provides for this. Art. II, sec. 3, says: ". . . he may, on extraordinary Occasions, convene both Houses, or either of them,"

Q. Can the Secretary of State take action with respect to recognizing a government without the consent of Congress?
A. The Secretary of State, on behalf of the President, may accord recognition without recourse to Congress (Art. II, sec. 3).

Q. Under the new government how was the national judiciary organized?
A. The First Congress passed many notable acts which endured many years as laws. One of the most worthy of these was that organizing the national judiciary, September 24, 1789. The bill was drawn up with extraordinary ability by Senator Oliver Ellsworth, of Connecticut, who had been a deputy to the Constitutional Convention, and who was to become Chief Justice of the United States. The Constitution prescribes a Supreme Court, but left its make-up and provision for other courts to Congress. The Supreme Court was organized with a Chief Justice and five Associates; a district court was provided for each State; and the Supreme Court Justices sat with the district judges in circuit courts. The jurisdiction of the three grades of the judiciary was fixed, and officers--clerks, marshals, and district attorneys--authorized. The Attorney General, also provided for in the act, was for many years little more than the President's legal adviser. Under this law President Washington appointed John Jay, of New York, Chief Justice, and the judiciary was organized on February 2, 1790.

Q. What are the correct style and titles of the Supreme Court of the United States and its members?
A. The correct title for the Supreme Court is "The Supreme Court of the United States"; for the members, one speaks of a Justice, or Associate Justice, of the Supreme Court of the United States, but always of the head of the court as "The Chief Justice of the United States" (Art. III, sec. I).

Q. What has been the number of Justices of the Supreme Court of the United States?
A. The Chief Justice is mentioned in the Constitution but the number of Justices is not specified. The act of September 24, 1789, provided for a Chief Justice and five Associates; that of February 24, 1807, made the Associates six; that of March 3, 1837, eight; and that of March 3, 1863, nine. But on July 23, 1866, a law directed that no appointments be made of Associate Justices until the number of them should be only six. This was to prevent President Johnson from making appointments; but the act of April 10, 1869, restored the number to eight. There were only six at the time that President Grant made the first restorative appointments.

Q. It is frequently asserted that the Supreme Court nullifies an act of Congress. Is this correct?
A. No. The Court has repeatedly declared that it claims no such power. All it does--all it can do--is to examine a law when a suit is brought before it. If the law in question is in accordance with the Constitution, in

the opinion of the Supreme Court, the law stands. If the law goes beyond powers granted by the Constitution, then it is no law, and the Supreme Court merely states that fact (Art. III, sec. 2, cl. 1; Art. VI, cl. 2).

Q. In which decision did the Supreme Court first formally assert its authority contrary to an act of Congress?
A. In the famous case of Marbury v. Madison (1803). This was not the first case in which the authority of an act of Congress was questioned in a case before the court. In Hylton v. United States, 1796, the court upheld the constitutionality of a national tax on carriages as an excise that did not have to be apportioned. Also Justices in the circuit court had, as early as 1792, refused to act as commissioners under an act of Congress, considering the law unconstitutional.

Q. What is treason against the United States?
A. Treason against the United States consists in levying war against them, or in adhering to their enemies, giving the latter aid and comfort. No person can be convicted of treason except upon the testimony of two witnesses to the same overt act or on confession in open court (Art. III, sec. 3, cl. 1).

Q. What right has a Territorial Delegate in Congress?
A. A Territorial Delegate sits in the House of Representatives from each organized territory. Delegates may be appointed to committees and have the right to speak on any subject, but not to vote (Art. IV, sec. 3, cl. 2).

Q. Is a constitutional amendment submitted to the President?
A. No. A resolution proposing an amendment to the Constitution, after having passed both houses of Congress by a two-thirds vote, does not go to the President for his signature. It is sent to the States to be ratified either by their legislatures or by conventions, as Congress shall determine (Art. V). The Supreme Court as early as 1798 declared the approval was not requisite (Hollingsworth v. Virginia, 3 Dallas 378).

Q. What constitutes the supreme law of the land?
A. Art. VI, cl. 2 of the Constitution says: "This Constitution, and the Laws of the United States which shall be made in Pursuance thereof; and all Treaties made, or which shall be made, under the Authority of the United States, shalt be the supreme Law of the Land; and the Judges in every State shall be bound thereby, any Thing in the Constitution or Laws of any State to the Contrary notwithstanding."

Q. When referring to various States in the Union, is the term "sovereign States" correct?
A. No. A sovereign is that person or State which recognizes no superior. The States of the Union have a superior--the Constitution of the United States, which is "the supreme Law of the Land . . . any Thing in the Constitution or Laws of any State to the Contrary notwithstanding" (Art. VI, cl. 2).

Q. Is there a clause in the Constitution prohibiting members of certain religious denominations from becoming President of the United States?
A. No. Art. VI, cl. 3 of the Constitution provides that "no religious Test shall ever be required as a Qualification to any Office of public Trust under the United States."

Q. Should the amendments be called articles?
A. The amendments proposed by the first Congress were sent out as "Articles in addition to, and Amendment of the Constitution of the United States of America," and the term "article" is used in self-application in all the amendments since the Twelfth, except the Seventeenth, which uses the term "amendment." This would seem to give official sanction to calling the amendments "articles," but as it causes some confusion, they are better placed by the use of "amendment" only, with the proper number.

Q. In the first session of the First Congress how many proposed amendments were considered?
A. All of the amendments proposed by the State conventions were considered, but only approximately 90 separate amendments were formally introduced. Professor Ames lists 312 through the First Congress, which includes the 124 proposed by the States and all reports and amendments to those proposed, in Congress.

Q. Who proposed the creation of the first executive departments and the first amendments to the Constitution?
A. James Madison, of Virginia, proposed the resolutions for the formation of the first executive departments and the series of twelve amendments to the Constitution of which ten were finally ratified by the States.

Q. What constitutes the Bill of Rights?
A. The first ten amendments to the Constitution.

Q. It is said that when the first amendments to the Constitution were submitted, there were twelve, of which ten were adopted. What were the other two about?
A. The two amendments of the twelve submitted as the Bill of Rights which were rejected were the one which related to the apportionment of Representatives in Congress and the one fixing the compensation of members of Congress. (Note: The rejected second amendment was ratified on May 7,1992 as the 27th amendment.)

Q. Do the first ten amendments bind the States?
A. No. They restrict the powers of the national government. They do not bind the States; but various of their restrictions have been applied to the States by the Fourteenth Amendment.

Q. Does not the Constitution give us our rights and liberties?
A. No, it does not, it only guarantees them. The people had all their rights and liberties before they made the Constitution. The Constitution was formed, among other purposes, to make the people's liberties

secure—secure not only as against foreign attack but against oppression by their own government. They set specific limits upon their national government and upon the States, and reserved to themselves all powers that they did not grant. The Ninth Amendment declares: "The enumeration in the Constitution, of certain rights, shall not be construed to deny or disparage others retained by the people."

Q. What protection is given to a person accused of crime under the jurisdiction of the United States?
A. The Fifth Amendment declares that no person, except one serving in the land or naval forces or the militia in time of war or public danger, can be held to answer for a capital or other infamous crime unless on a presentment or indictment of a grand jury. No person can be twice put in jeopardy of life or limb for the same offense. No one in a criminal case can be compelled to be a witness against himself, or be deprived of life, liberty, or property without due process of law. Private property cannot be taken for public use without just compensation. By the Eighth Amendment excessive bail and fines and cruel and unusual punishments are prohibited. The original Constitution forbids ex post facto laws and bills of attainder, limits the punishment for treason, protects the right to a writ of habeas corpus, and secures trial by jury.

Q. Is the right to speedy trial guaranteed?
A. Yes. The Sixth Amendment expressly states that in all criminal prosecutions the accused shall enjoy the right to a speedy and public trial by an impartial jury within the district of the crime, and to be informed of the nature and cause of the accusation. He is entitled to be confronted with the witnesses against him, to be allowed to compel the attendance of witnesses in his favor, and to have the assistance of counsel for his defense.

Q. Is the right of trial by jury in civil cases also assured?
A. Yes. Amendment Seven preserves the right of trial by jury in suits of common law involving the value of more than twenty dollars.

Q. What has been the longest period during which no amendment has been added to the Constitution?
A. Sixty-one years, from 1804 to 1865. This period elapsed between the Twelfth and Thirteenth Amendments.

Q. How long did it take the States to ratify the income tax amendment?
A. The Sixteenth Amendment was proposed to the States on July 12, 1909, deposited with the Secretary of State on July 21, ratified by the thirty-sixth state on February 3, 1913, and, declared ratified on February 25, 1913.

Q. It has been stated that the Prohibition Amendment was the first instance of incorporating a statute in the Constitution. Is this so?
A. No. Those portions of the Constitution which specifically dealt with slavery and the slave trade (Art. I, sec. 9, cl. 1; Art. IV, sec. 2, cl. 3) were both of this character. They were made obsolete by time limit in one case and the Civil War in the other.

Q. How many amendments to the Constitution have been repealed?
A. Only one -- the Eighteenth (Prohibition).

Q. How is an amendment repealed?
A. By adding another amendment.

Q. If the Eighteenth Amendment is repealed, why is it necessary to call the new one repealing it the Twenty-first?
A. The Eighteenth Amendment will indeed remain in the Constitution, but a notation will be added to the effect that it is repealed by the Twenty-first.

Q. What is the Twentieth Amendment and when was it adopted?
A. This is the so-called "Lame Duck" Amendment, which changes the time for the beginning of the terms of the President, Vice President, and the members of Congress. The term of the President and Vice President begins on January 20, and that of members of Congress on January 3. It was adopted upon the ratification by the thirty-sixth State, January 23, 1933, and certified in effect on February 6.

Q. Why was a constitutional amendment necessary to change the date of the beginning of the terms of President, Vice President, and members of Congress?
A. The Constitution fixes the terms of President and, Vice President at four years, of Senators at six years, and of Representatives at two years. Any change of date would affect the terms of the incumbents. It was therefore necessary to amend the Constitution to make the change.

Q. If the President-elect dies, who becomes President at the beginning of the term for which he was elected?
A. The Twentieth Amendment provides that in this case the Vice President-elect shall become President.

Q. Does the Twentieth Amendment do away with the Electoral College?
A. It does not.

Q. It takes how many States to block an amendment?
A. Thirteen,

Part VII: Appendices – Founding Documents

Appendix A: The Declaration of Rights and Grievances

At the First Continental Congress, the delegates drafted several documents, and several drafts of documents, one of which was the Declaration of Rights and Grievances. This was a statement of American complaints. It was sent to King George III, to whom, at the time, many of the delegates remained loyal. It was not sent to Parliament since the delegates did not have the same level of loyalty to this body. Quite frankly, The document implored King George III to step in and rescue the colonies from the English Parliament.

The radical delegates were critical of this particular *Declaration* because it continued to concede the right of Parliament to regulate colonial trade, a view that was losing favor in the mid-1770s. Many suggest that the actual cause of the American Revolution is found in this major historical document.

The full text of the Declaration of Rights and Grievances along with proper explanations is displayed in Chapter 9 and is not repeated in this Appendix.

Appendix B
The Articles of Association

Articles of Association stated that if the Intolerable Acts were not repealed by December 1, 1774, a boycott of British goods would begin in the colonies. The full text of the Articles of Association along with proper explanations is in Chapter 10 and is not repeated in this Appendix.

Appendix C
The Declaration of Independence

On July 4, 1776, the Second Continental Congress, announced that the thirteen American colonies, then at war with Great Britain, regarded themselves as 13 newly independent sovereign states, and no longer a part of the British Empire. The full text of the Declaration of Independence along with proper explanations is displayed in Chapter 11 and is not repeated in this Appendix.

Appendix D
The Articles of Confederation

The Articles of Confederation was an agreement among the 13 founding states that established the United States of America as a confederation of sovereign states and served as its first constitution. The full text of the Articles of Confederation with proper explanations is displayed in Chapter 12 and is not repeated in this Appendix.

Appendix E
The US Constitution America

The Constitution of the United States is the supreme law of the United States of America. The Constitution, originally comprising seven articles, delineates the national frame of government. The full text of the Constitution of the United States of America along with proper explanations is displayed in Chapter 13 and is not repeated in this appendix.

Appendix F
The Bill of Rights & Other Constitutional Amendments

The first ten amendments to the U.S. Constitution are known as The Bill of Rights. Freedom of religion, speech, press, assembly, and petition. Right to keep and bear arms in order to maintain a well regulated militia. A full explanation is displayed in Chapter 14. The full text of the seventeen amendments is contained in this Appendix.

The Constitution: Amendments 11-27

Constitutional Amendments 1-10 make up what is known as The Bill of Rights. Amendments 11-27 are listed below.

AMENDMENT XI
Passed by Congress March 4, 1794. Ratified February 7, 1795.
Note: Article III, section 2, of the Constitution was modified by amendment 11.
The Judicial power of the United States shall not be construed to extend to any suit in law or equity, commenced or prosecuted against one of the United States by Citizens of another State, or by Citizens or Subjects of any Foreign State.

AMENDMENT XII
Passed by Congress December 9, 1803. Ratified June 15, 1804.

Note: A portion of Article II, section 1 of the Constitution was superseded by the 12th amendment.

The Electors shall meet in their respective states and vote by ballot for President and Vice-President, one of whom, at least, shall not be an inhabitant of the same state with themselves; they shall name in their ballots the person voted for as President, and in distinct ballots the person voted for as Vice-President, and they shall make distinct lists of all persons voted for as President, and of all persons voted for as Vice-President, and of the number of votes for each, which lists they shall sign and certify, and transmit sealed to the seat of the government of the United States, directed to the President of the Senate; -- the President of the Senate shall, in the presence of the Senate and House of Representatives, open all the certificates and the votes shall then be counted; -- The person having the greatest number of votes for President, shall be the President, if such number be a majority of the whole number of Electors appointed; and if no person have such majority, then from the persons having the highest numbers not exceeding three on the list of those voted for as President, the House of Representatives shall choose immediately, by ballot, the President. But in choosing the President, the votes shall be taken by states, the representation from each state having one vote; a quorum for this purpose shall consist of a member or members from two-thirds of the states, and a majority of all the states shall be necessary to a choice.
[And if the House of Representatives shall not choose a President whenever the right of choice shall devolve upon them, before the fourth day of March next following, then the Vice-President shall act as President, as in case of the death or other constitutional disability of the President. --]* The person having the greatest number of votes as Vice-President, shall be the Vice-President, if such number be a majority of the whole number of Electors appointed, and if no person have a majority, then from the two highest numbers on the list, the Senate shall choose the Vice-President; a quorum for the purpose shall consist of two-thirds of the whole number of Senators, and a majority of the whole number shall be necessary to a choice. But no person constitutionally ineligible to the office of President shall be eligible to that of Vice-President of the United States.

*Later Superseded by section 3 of the 20th amendment.

AMENDMENT XIII
Passed by Congress January 31, 1865. Ratified December 6, 1865.

Note: A portion of Article IV, section 2, of the Constitution was superseded by the 13th amendment.

Section 1.
Neither slavery nor involuntary servitude, except as a punishment for crime whereof the party shall have been duly convicted, shall exist within the United States, or any place subject to their jurisdiction.

Section 2.
Congress shall have power to enforce this article by appropriate legislation.

AMENDMENT XIV
Passed by Congress June 13, 1866. Ratified July 9, 1868.
Note: Article I, section 2, of the Constitution was modified by section 2 of the 14th amendment.

Section 1.
All persons born or naturalized in the United States, and subject to the jurisdiction thereof, are citizens of the United States and of the State wherein they reside. No State shall make or enforce any law which shall abridge the privileges or immunities of citizens of the United States; nor shall any State deprive any person of life, liberty, or property, without due process of law; nor deny to any person within its jurisdiction the equal protection of the laws.

Section 2.
Representatives shall be apportioned among the several States according to their respective numbers, counting the whole number of persons in each State, excluding Indians not taxed. But when the right to vote at any election for the choice of electors for President and Vice-President of the United States, Representatives in Congress, the Executive and Judicial officers of a State, or the members of the Legislature thereof, is denied to any of the male inhabitants of such State, being twenty-one years of age,* and citizens of the United States, or in any way abridged, except for participation in rebellion, or other crime, the basis of representation therein shall be reduced in the proportion which the number of such male citizens shall bear to the whole number of male citizens twenty-one years of age in such State.

Section 3.
No person shall be a Senator or Representative in Congress, or elector of President and Vice-President, or hold any office, civil or military, under the United States, or under any State, who, having previously taken an oath, as a member of Congress, or as an officer of the United States, or as a member of any State legislature, or as an executive or judicial officer of any State, to support the Constitution of the United States, shall have engaged in insurrection or rebellion against the same, or given aid or comfort to the enemies thereof. But Congress may by a vote of two-thirds of each House, remove such disability.

Section 4.
The validity of the public debt of the United States, authorized by law, including debts incurred for payment of pensions and bounties for services in suppressing insurrection or rebellion, shall not be questioned. But neither the United States nor any State shall assume or pay any debt or obligation incurred in aid of insurrection or rebellion against the United States, or any claim for the loss or emancipation of any slave; but all such debts, obligations and claims shall be held illegal and void.

Section 5.
The Congress shall have the power to enforce, by appropriate legislation, the provisions of this article.

*Later Changed by section 1 of the 26th amendment.

AMENDMENT XV
Passed by Congress February 26, 1869. Ratified February 3, 1870.

Section 1.
The right of citizens of the United States to vote shall not be denied or abridged by the United States or by any State on account of race, color, or previous condition of servitude--

Section 2.
The Congress shall have the power to enforce this article by appropriate legislation.

AMENDMENT XVI
Passed by Congress July 2, 1909. Ratified February 3, 1913.
Note: Article I, section 9, of the Constitution was modified by amendment 16.
The Congress shall have power to lay and collect taxes on incomes, from whatever source derived, without apportionment among the several States, and without regard to any census or enumeration.

AMENDMENT XVII
Passed by Congress May 13, 1912. Ratified April 8, 1913.
Note: Article I, section 3, of the Constitution was modified by the 17th amendment.
---The Senate of the United States shall be composed of two Senators from each State, elected by the people thereof, for six years; and each Senator shall have one vote. The electors in each State shall have the qualifications requisite for electors of the most numerous branch of the State legislatures.
---When vacancies happen in the representation of any State in the Senate, the executive authority of such State shall issue writs of election to fill such vacancies: Provided, That the legislature of any State may empower the executive thereof to make temporary appointments until the people fill the vacancies by election as the legislature may direct.
---This amendment shall not be so construed as to affect the election or term of any Senator chosen before it becomes valid as part of the Constitution.

AMENDMENT XVIII
Passed by Congress December 18, 1917. Ratified January 16, 1919. Repealed by amendment 21.

Section 1.
After one year from the ratification of this article the manufacture, sale, or transportation of intoxicating liquors within, the importation thereof into, or the exportation thereof from the United States and all territory subject to the jurisdiction thereof for beverage purposes is hereby prohibited.

Section 2.
The Congress and the several States shall have concurrent power to enforce this article by appropriate legislation.

Section 3.
This article shall be inoperative unless it shall have been ratified as an amendment to the Constitution by the legislatures of the several States, as provided in the Constitution, within seven years from the date of the submission hereof to the States by the Congress.

AMENDMENT XIX
Passed by Congress June 4, 1919. Ratified August 18, 1920.
The right of citizens of the United States to vote shall not be denied or abridged by the United States or by any State on account of sex.
Congress shall have power to enforce this article by appropriate legislation.

AMENDMENT XX
Passed by Congress March 2, 1932. Ratified January 23, 1933.
Note: Article I, section 4, of the Constitution was modified by section 2 of this amendment. In addition, a portion of the 12th amendment was superseded by section 3.

Section 1.
The terms of the President and the Vice President shall end at noon on the 20th day of January, and the terms of Senators and Representatives at noon on the 3d day of January, of the years in which such terms would have ended if this article had not been ratified; and the terms of their successors shall then begin.

Section 2.
The Congress shall assemble at least once in every year, and such meeting shall begin at noon on the 3d day of January, unless they shall by law appoint a different day.

Section 3.
If, at the time fixed for the beginning of the term of the President, the President elect shall have died, the Vice President elect shall become President. If a President shall not have been chosen before the time fixed for the beginning of his term, or if the President elect shall have failed to qualify, then the Vice President elect shall act as President until a President shall have qualified; and the Congress may by law provide for the case wherein neither a President elect nor a Vice President shall have qualified, declaring who shall then act as President, or the manner in which one who is to act shall be selected, and such

person shall act accordingly until a President or Vice President shall have qualified.

Section 4
The Congress may by law provide for the case of the death of any of the persons from whom the House of Representatives may choose a President whenever the right of choice shall have devolved upon them, and for the case of the death of any of the persons from whom the Senate may choose a Vice President whenever the right of choice shall have devolved upon them.

Section 5.
Sections 1 and 2 shall take effect on the 15th day of October following the ratification of this article.

Section 6.
This article shall be inoperative unless it shall have been ratified as an amendment to the Constitution by the legislatures of three-fourths of the several States within seven years from the date of its submission.

AMENDMENT XXI
Passed by Congress February 20, 1933. Ratified December 5, 1933.
Section 1.
The eighteenth article of amendment to the Constitution of the United States is hereby repealed.

Section 2.
The transportation or importation into any State, Territory, or Possession of the United States for delivery or use therein of intoxicating liquors, in violation of the laws thereof, is hereby prohibited.

Section 3.
This article shall be inoperative unless it shall have been ratified as an amendment to the Constitution by conventions in the several States, as provided in the Constitution, within seven years from the date of the submission hereof to the States by the Congress.

AMENDMENT XXII
Passed by Congress March 21, 1947. Ratified February 27, 1951.
Section 1.
No person shall be elected to the office of the President more than twice, and no person who has held the office of President, or acted as President, for more than two years of a term to which some other person was elected President shall be elected to the office of President more than once. But this Article shall not apply to any person holding the office of President when this Article was proposed by Congress, and shall not prevent any person who may be holding the office of President, or acting as President, during the term within which this Article becomes operative from holding the office of President or acting as President during the remainder of such term.

Section 2.
This article shall be inoperative unless it shall have been ratified as an amendment to the Constitution by the legislatures of three-fourths of the several States within seven years from the date of its submission to the States by the Congress.

AMENDMENT XXIII
Passed by Congress June 16, 1960. Ratified March 29, 1961.

Section 1.
The District constituting the seat of Government of the United States shall appoint in such manner as Congress may direct:
---A number of electors of President and Vice President equal to the whole number of Senators and Representatives in Congress to which the District would be entitled if it were a State, but in no event more than the least populous State; they shall be in addition to those appointed by the States, but they shall be considered, for the purposes of the election of President and Vice President, to be electors appointed by a State; and they shall meet in the District and perform such duties as provided by the twelfth article of amendment.
Section 2.
The Congress shall have power to enforce this article by appropriate legislation.

AMENDMENT XXIV
Passed by Congress August 27, 1962. Ratified January 23, 1964.
Section 1.
The right of citizens of the United States to vote in any primary or other election for President or Vice President, for electors for President or Vice President, or for Senator or Representative in Congress, shall not be denied or abridged by the United States or any State by reason of failure to pay poll tax or other tax.

Section 2.
The Congress shall have power to enforce this article by appropriate legislation.

AMENDMENT XXV
Passed by Congress July 6, 1965. Ratified February 10, 1967.
Note: Article II, section 1, of the Constitution was affected by the 25th amendment.

Section 1.
In case of the removal of the President from office or of his death or resignation, the Vice President shall become President.

Section 2.
Whenever there is a vacancy in the office of the Vice President, the President shall nominate a Vice President who shall take office upon confirmation by a majority vote of both Houses of Congress.

Section 3.
Whenever the President transmits to the President pro tempore of the Senate and the Speaker of the House of Representatives his written declaration that he

is unable to discharge the powers and duties of his office, and until he transmits to them a written declaration to the contrary, such powers and duties shall be discharged by the Vice President as Acting President.

Section 4.
Whenever the Vice President and a majority of either the principal officers of the executive departments or of such other body as Congress may by law provide, transmit to the President pro tempore of the Senate and the Speaker of the House of Representatives their written declaration that the President is unable to discharge the powers and duties of his office, the Vice President shall immediately assume the powers and duties of the office as Acting President. ---Thereafter, when the President transmits to the President pro tempore of the Senate and the Speaker of the House of Representatives his written declaration that no inability exists, he shall resume the powers and duties of his office unless the Vice President and a majority of either the principal officers of the executive department or of such other body as Congress may by law provide, transmit within four days to the President pro tempore of the Senate and the Speaker of the House of Representatives their written declaration that the President is unable to discharge the powers and duties of his office. Thereupon Congress shall decide the issue, assembling within forty-eight hours for that purpose if not in session. If the Congress, within twenty-one days after receipt of the latter written declaration, or, if Congress is not in session, within twenty-one days after Congress is required to assemble, determines by two-thirds vote of both Houses that the President is unable to discharge the powers and duties of his office, the Vice President shall continue to discharge the same as Acting President; otherwise, the President shall resume the powers and duties of his office.

AMENDMENT XXVI
Passed by Congress March 23, 1971. Ratified July 1, 1971.
Note: Amendment 14, section 2, of the Constitution was modified by section 1 of the 26th amendment.

Section 1.
The right of citizens of the United States, who are eighteen years of age or older, to vote shall not be denied or abridged by the United States or by any State on account of age.

Section 2.
The Congress shall have power to enforce this article by appropriate legislation.

AMENDMENT XXVII
Originally proposed Sept. 25, 1789. Ratified May 7, 1992.
No law, varying the compensation for the services of the Senators and Representatives, shall take effect, until an election of representatives shall have intervened.
http://www.archives.gov/national-archives-experience/charters/constitution_amendments_11-27.html

Appendix G
Constitutional Amendments Not Ratified

These are the proposed amendments to the Constitution—not ratified by the States.

During the course of our history, in addition to the 27 amendments that have been ratified by the required three-fourths of the States, six other amendments have been submitted to the States but have not been ratified by them.

Beginning with the proposed Eighteenth Amendment, Congress has customarily included a provision requiring ratification within seven years from the time of the submission to the States. The Supreme Court in Coleman v. Miller, 307 U.S. 433 (1939), declared that the question of the reasonableness of the time within which a sufficient number of States must act is a political question to be determined by the Congress.

In 1789, twelve proposed articles of amendment were submitted to the States. Of these, Articles III through XII were ratified and became the first ten amendments to the Constitution, popularly known as the Bill of Rights. In 1992, proposed Article II was ratified and became the 27th amendment to the Constitution. Proposed Article I which was not ratified is as follows:

"Article the first"

> "After the first enumeration required by the first article of the Constitution, there shall be one Representative for every thirty thousand, until the number shall amount to one hundred, after which the proportion shall be so regulated by Congress, that there shall be not less than one hundred Representatives, nor less than one Representative for every forty thousand persons, until the number of Representatives shall amount to two hundred; after which the proportion shall be so regulated by Congress, that there shall not be less than two hundred Representatives, nor more than one Representative for every fifty thousand persons."

Thereafter, in the 2d session of the Eleventh Congress, the Congress proposed the following article of amendment to the Constitution relating to acceptance by citizens of the United States of titles of nobility from any foreign government.

The proposed amendment, which was not ratified by three-fourths of the States, is as follows:

Resolved by the Senate and House of Representatives of the United States of America in Congress assembled, two thirds of both houses concurring, That the following section be submitted to the legislatures of the several states, which, when ratified by the legislatures of three fourths of the states, shall be valid and binding, as a part of the constitution of the United States.

> If any citizen of the United States shall accept, claim, receive or retain any title of nobility or honour, or shall, without the consent of Congress, accept and retain any present, pension, office or emolument of any kind whatever, from any emperor, king, prince or foreign power, such person shall cease to be a citizen of the United States, and shall be incapable of holding any office of trust or profit under them, or either of them.

The following amendment to the Constitution relating to slavery was proposed by the 2d session of the Thirty-sixth Congress on March 2, 1861, when it passed the Senate, having previously passed the House on February 28, 1861. It is interesting to note in this connection that this is the only proposed (and not ratified) amendment to the Constitution to have been signed by the President. The President's signature is considered unnecessary because of the constitutional provision that on the concurrence of two-thirds of both Houses of Congress the proposal shall be submitted to the States for ratification.

> Resolved by the Senate and House of Representatives of the United States of America in Congress assembled, That the following article be proposed to the Legislatures of the several States as an amendment to the Constitution of the United States, which, when ratified by three-fourths of said Legislatures, shall be valid, to all intents and purposes, as part of the said Constitution, viz:
>
> **"Article Thirteen**
>
> "No amendment shall be made to the Constitution which will authorize or give to Congress the power to abolish or interfere, within any State, with the domestic institutions thereof, including that of persons held to labor or service by the laws of said State."

A child labor amendment was proposed by the 1st session of the Sixty-eighth Congress on June 2, 1926, when it passed the Senate, having previously passed the House on April 26, 1926. The proposed amendment, which has been ratified by 28 States, to date, is as follows:

Joint Resolution Proposing an Amendment to the Constitution of the United States

> Resolved by the Senate and House of Representatives of the United States of America in Congress assembled (two-thirds of each House concurring therein), That the following article is proposed as an amendment to the Constitution of the United States, which, when ratified by the legislatures of three-fourths of the several States, shall be valid to all intents and purposes as a part of the Constitution:
>
> **"Article—[no number given].**
>
> "Section 1. The Congress shall have power to limit, regulate, and prohibit the labor of persons under eighteen years of age.
>
> "Section 2. The power of the several States is unimpaired by this article except that the operation of State laws shall be suspended to the extent necessary to give effect to legislation enacted by the Congress."

HOUSE JOINT RESOLUTION 208

An amendment relative to equal rights for men and women was proposed by the 2d session of the Ninety-second Congress on March 22, 1972, when it passed the Senate, having previously passed the House on October 12, 1971. The seven-year deadline for ratification of the proposed amendment was extended to June 30, 1982, by the 2d session of the Ninety-fifth Congress. The proposed amendment, which was not ratified by three-fourths of the States by June 30, 1982, is as follows:

Joint Resolution Proposing an Amendment to the Constitution of the United States Relative to Equal Rights for Men and Women

Resolved by the Senate and House of Representatives of the United States of America in Congress assembled (two-thirds of each House concurring therein), That the following article is proposed as an amendment to the Constitution of the United States, which shall be valid to all intents and purposes as part of the Constitution when ratified by the legislatures of three-fourths of the several States within seven years from the date of its submission by the Congress:

"Article—[No number given]

"Section 1. Equality of rights under the law shall not be denied or abridged by the United States or by any State on account of sex.

"Section. 2. The Congress shall have the power to enforce, by appropriate legislation, the provisions of this article.

"Section. 3. This amendment shall take effect two years after the date of ratification."

HOUSE JOINT RESOLUTION 554

An amendment relative to voting rights for the District of Columbia was proposed by the 2d session of the Ninety-fifth Congress on August 22, 1978, when it passed the Senate, having previously passed the House on March 2, 1978. The proposed amendment, which was not ratified by three-fourths of the States within the specified seven-year period, is as follows:

Joint Resolution Proposing an Amendment to the Constitution To Provide for Representation of the District of Columbia in the Congress

Resolved by the Senate and House of Representatives of the United States of America in Congress assembled (two-thirds of each House concurring therein), That the following article is proposed as an amendment to the Constitution of the United States, which shall be valid to all intents and purposes as part of the Constitution when ratified by the legislatures of three-fourths of the several States within seven years from the date of its submission by the Congress:

"Article—[No number given]

"Section 1. For purposes of representation in the Congress, election of the President and Vice President, and article V of this Constitution, the District constituting the seat of government of the United States shall be treated as though it were a State.

"Section. 2. The exercise of the rights and powers conferred under this article shall be by the people of the District constituting the seat of government, and as shall be provided by the Congress.

"Section. 3. The twenty-third article of amendment to the Constitution of the United States is hereby repealed.

"Section. 4. This article shall be inoperative, unless it shall have been ratified as an amendment to the Constitution by the legislatures of three-fourths of the several States within seven years from the date of its submission."

The End of *The Constitution 4 Dummmies!*

Thank you for your attention!

LETS GO PUBLISH! Books by

Brian Kelly: (sold at www.bookhawkers.com Amazon.com,

and Kindle.).

LETS GO PUBLISH! is proud to announce that more AS/400 and Power i books are becoming available to help you inexpensively address your AS/400 and Power i education and training needs: Our general titles precede specific AS/400 and other technology books.

Why Trump?
You Already Know… But, this book will tell you anyway

Saving America The Trump Way!
A book that tells you how President Donald Trump will help Merica dn Americans wind up on top

The US Immigration Fix
It's all in here. You won't want to put it down

Great Moments in Penn State Football Check out the particulars of this great book at bookhawkers.com.

Great Moments in Notre Dame Football Check out the particulars of this great book at bookhawkers.com or www.notredamebooks.com

WineDiets.Com Presents The Wine Diet Learn how to lose weight while having fun. Four specific diets and some great anecdotes fill this book with fun and the opportunity to lose weight in the process.

Wilkes-Barre, PA; Return to Glory Wilkes-Barre City's return to glory begins with dreams and ideas. Along with plans and actions, this equals leadership.

The Lifetime Guest Plan. This is a plan which if deployed today would immediately solve the problem of 60 million illegal aliens in the United States.

Geoffrey Parsons' Epoch... The Land of Fair Play Better than the original. The greatest re-mastering of the greatest book ever written on American Civics. It was built for all Americans as the best govt. design in the history of the world.

The Bill of Rights 4 Dummmies! This is the best book to learn about your rights. Be the first, to have a "Rights Fest" on your block. You will win for sure!

Sol Bloom's Epoch ...Story of the Constitution This work by Sol Bloom was written to commemorate the Sesquicentennial celebration of the Constitution. It has been remastered by Lets Go Publish! – An excellent read!

The Constitution 4 Dummmies! This is the best book to learn about the Constitution. Learn all about the fundamental laws of America.

America for Dummmies!
All Americans should read to learn about this great country.

Just Say No to Chris Christie for President!
Discusses the reasons why Chris Christie is a poor choice for US President

The Federalist Papers by Hamilton, Jay, Madison w/ intro by Brian Kelly
Complete unabridged, easier to read version of the original Federalist Papers

Kill the Republican Party!
Demonstrates why the Republican Party must be abandoned by conservatives

Bring On the American Party!
Demonstrates how conservatives can be free from the party of wimps by starting its own national party called the American Party.

No Amnesty! No Way!
In addition to describing the issue in detail, this book also offers a real solution.

Saving America
This how-to book is about saving our country using strong mercantilist principles. These same principles that helped the country from its founding.

RRR:
A unique plan for economic recovery and job creation

Kill the EPA
The EPA seems to hate mankind and love nature. They are also making it tough for asthmatics to breathe and for those with malaria to live. It's time they go.

Obama's Seven Deadly Sins.
In the Obama Presidency, there are many concerns about the long-term prospects and sustainability of the country. We examine each of the President's seven deadliest sins in detail, offering warnings and a number of solutions. Be careful. Book may nudge you to move to Canada or Europe.

Taxation Without Representation Second Edition
At the time of the Boston Tea Party, there was no representation. Now, there is no representation again but there are "representatives."

Healthcare Accountability
Who should pay for your healthcare? Whose healthcare should you pay for? Is it a lifetime free ride on others or should those once in need of help have to pay it back when their lives improve?

Jobs! Jobs! Jobs!
Where have all the American Jobs gone and how can we get them back?

Other IBM I Technical Books

The All Everything Operating System:
Story about IBM's finest operating system; its facilities; how it came to be.

The All-Everything Machine
Story about IBM's finest computer server.

Chip Wars
The story of ongoing wars between Intel and AMD and upcoming wars between Intel and IBM. Book may cause you to buy / sell somebody's stock.

Can the AS/400 Survive IBM?
Exciting book about the AS/400 in a System i5 World.

The IBM i Pocket SQL Guide.
Complete Pocket Guide to SQL as implemented on System i5. A must have for SQL developers new to System i5. It is very compact yet very comprehensive and it is example driven. Written in a part tutorial and part reference style, Tons of SQL coding samples, from the simple to the sublime.

The IBM i Pocket Query Guide.
If you have been spending money for years educating your Query users, and you find you are still spending, or you've given up, this book is right for you. This one QuikCourse covers all Query options.

The IBM I Pocket RPG & RPG IV Guide.
Comprehensive RPG & RPGIV Textbook -- Over 900 pages. This is the one RPG book to have if you are not having more than one. All areas of the language covered smartly in a convenient sized book Annotated PowerPoint's available for self-study (extra fee for self-study package)

The IBM I RPG Tutorial and Lab Guide – Recently Revised.
Your guide to a hands-on Lab experience. Contains CD with Lab exercises and PowerPoint's. Great companion to the above textbook or can be used as a standalone for student Labs or tutorial purposes

The IBM i Pocket Developers' Guide.
Comprehensive Pocket Guide to all of the AS/400 and System i5 development tools - DFU, SDA, etc. You'll also get a big bonus with chapters on Architecture, Work Management, and Subfile Coding.

The IBM i Pocket Database Guide.
Complete Pocket Guide to System i5 integrated relational database (DB2/400) – physical and logical files and DB operations - Union, Projection, Join, etc. Written in a part tutorial and part reference style. Tons of DDS coding samples.

Getting Started with The WebSphere Development Studio Client for System i5 (WDSc). Focus is on client server and the Web. Includes CODE/400, VisualAge RPG, CGI, WebFacing, and WebSphere Studio. Case study continues from the Interactive Book.

The System i5 Pocket WebFacing Primer.
This book gets you started immediately with WebFacing. A sample case study is used as the basis for a conversion to WebFacing. Interactive 5250 application is WebFaced in a case study form before your eyes.

Getting Started with WebSphere Express Server for IBM i Step-by-Step Guide for Setting up Express Servers
A comprehensive guide to setting up and using WebSphere Express. It is filled with examples, and structured in a tutorial fashion for easy learning.

The WebFacing Application Design & Development Guide:
Step by Step Guide to designing green screen IBM i apps for the Web. Both a systems design guide and a developers guide. Book helps you understand how to design and develop Web applications using regular RPG or COBOL programs.

The System i5 Express Web Implementer's Guide. Your one stop guide to ordering, installing, fixing, configuring, and using WebSphere Express, Apache, WebFacing, System i5 Access for Web, and HATS/LE.

Joomla! Technical Books

Best Damn Joomla Tutorial Ever
Learn Joomla! By example.

Best Damn Joomla Intranet Tutorial Ever
This book is the only book that shows you how to use Joomla on a corporate intranet.

Best Damn Joomla Template Tutorial Ever
This book teaches you step-by step how to work with templates in Joomla!

Best Damn Joomla Installation Guide Ever
Teaches you how to install Joomla! On all major platforms besides IBM i.

Best Damn Blueprint for Building Your Own Corporate Intranet.
This excellent timeless book helps you design a corporate intranet for any platform while using Joomla as its basis.

IBM i PHP & MySQL Installation & Operations Guide
How to install and operate Joomla! on the IBM i Platform

IBM i PHP & MySQL Programmers Guide
How to write PHP and MySQL programs for IBM i

www.ingramcontent.com/pod-product-compliance
Lightning Source LLC
Chambersburg PA
CBHW072116270326
41931CB00010B/1574